Adventure and Environmental Activities

Chris Eksteen

Published by Panza Publishers
Panzabyte (PTY) LTD
Reg. No. 2009/020295/07
Koppiesvlei 518, Theunissen, 9410
Free State, South Africa

Copyright of text © 2016 by Chris Eksteen
Copyright of cover and illustrations © 2016 by Corné Botha
Copyright of pictures and graphics © 2016 by Koppiesvlei Outdoor Education Centre

All rights reserved.

No part of this publication may be reproduced, distributed, or transmitted in any form or by any means, or stored in a database or retrieval system without the prior written permission of the author.

Edited by Suzanne Opperman-Kemp and Natáscha Strauss
Cover by Corné Botha
Illustrations by Corné Botha
Proofread by Leon Sebastian Swart

Photographs were taken at Koppiesvlei Outdoor Education Centre
Printed and bound by Mega Digital in South Africa and CreateSpace in the United States of America, United Kingdom, France, Italy, Japan, New Zealand, Australia, et cetera.

First edition, first print 2016
First edition, second print 2019

ISBN: 978-0-9946935-8-7 (softcover)
ISBN: 978-0-9946935-9-4 (ePub)
ISBN: 978-0-9946936-0-0 (PDF)

This book is dedicated to my mentor and great friend, Nic Shaw.
Thank you for moulding me at my career roots.

In every walk with nature one receives far more than he seeks.
JOHN MUIR

Contents

Preface	1
Morning Activities	3
Day Activities	9
Evening Activities	55
Environmental Activities	79
Camping Out	93

Preface

This fourth book in the *Outdoor Education Resource Series* supplements the team building activities in the third book, "Group Dynamics: Icebreakers, Team Building and Leadership Exercises", with adventure and environmental activities.

With this book, I hope to once again provide newcomers to the industry with a starting point for dealing with groups and keeping them busy. While it is not a complete guide of all the activities in the industry, the book provides my view and understanding of selected activities and will be helpful to group guides of all levels of experience.

My sincere gratitude goes out to the talented Corné Botha for the lovely cover of this book. Your work truly inspires those around you. I would also like to thank Suzanne Opperman-Kemp and Natáscha Strauss for editing the manuscript with so much care and providing support throughout the production of the series.

Last, but certainly not least, I would like to thank all of my readers and followers. Without you, this series would not have seen the light. Thank you!

Regards
Chris Eksteen
2016

Morning Activities

Cow Milking

Preparation:
- Arrange a day and time for a milking session with the staff of a nearby milking farm.
- You will need:
    - Milking cream
    - 1 bucket

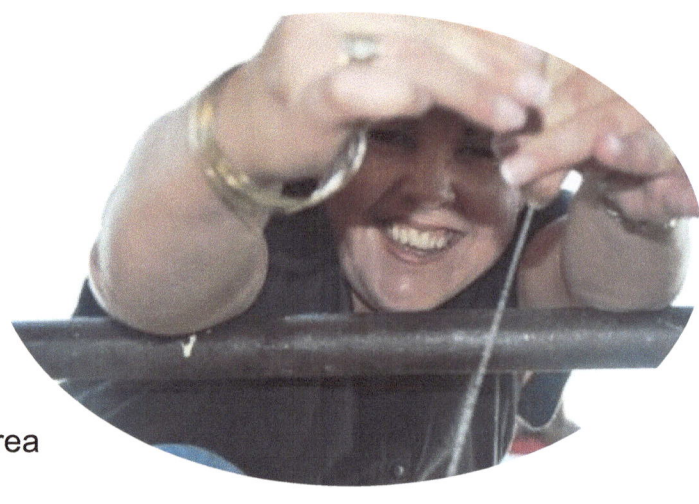

Site:
- At the farm or, if possible, in a safe area on the campsite, e.g. a shed or pen.

How it works:
- Take the group to the milking site and let them stand in an open area, not too close to the cows.
- Only two group members are allowed to approach the cows at a time.
- No loud noises are allowed.
- Moisten the group members' thumbs and forefingers slightly with milking cream.
- Kneel down with the group members and show them how to milk:
    - Moisten the teats evenly with the milking cream.
    - Take hold of the top part of the teat, with a thumb in front and two other fingers behind the teat.
    - Gently squeeze the teat while sliding your fingers down to the very tip in order to get the milk into the bucket.
    - Give the teat about half a second to fill up again and repeat the process.
- Allow each group member to milk a teat two or three times, and then move on to the next person.

Safety:
- Never stand or walk behind a cow – it may kick you.
- Do not poke the cows.
- Ensure that there are no safety hazards in the area.

After the session:
- Discuss the uses of milk with the group, e.g. cheese, yoghurt, etc.
- If time allows, let smaller kids colour in a picture of a cow, or a mouse with cheese.
- Wash the bucket and put it away, along with the milking cream.

Solitaire

You will need:
- 1 pencil per person
- 1 x A5 solitaire sheet per person (make copies of the solitaire sheet following these instructions)
- 1 pressing board per person (to press on while writing)

Site:
- Somewhere quiet and very spacious.

How it works:
- This activity gives each group member time to reflect by themselves.
- Allow about 45 minutes to an hour for this activity.
- At a Christian camp, open and close the activity with Scripture and prayer.
- This activity can also be used as a creative writing exercise.
- Instruct the group members to split up and find a quiet spot to sit by themselves, at least 10 m away from the rest of the group.
- Once they have found their spot, each group member must complete the solitaire sheet.
- The questions asked on the solitaire sheet are confidential and won't be shared with the rest of the group.
- Everyone must be quiet and try not to disturb one another – no talking is allowed.
- Group members are not allowed to get up and walk around.
- Even if they have finished before the allocated time, they must sit quietly and wait to be called back.

After the session:
- Ask the group if they would like to share any thoughts from their reflective time.
- Collect and put away all the equipment.

Solitaire

Your name: _____
Campsite: _____

It may be hard for an egg to turn into a bird: it would be a jolly sight harder for a bird to learn to fly while remaining an egg. We are like eggs at present. And you cannot go on indefinitely being just an ordinary, decent egg. We must be hatched or go bad.

C.S. LEWIS

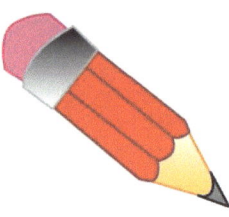

Sit somewhere on your own and . . . RELAX!

Write down three words that best describe the way you are feeling now:

1. _____
2. _____
3. _____

Now sit back and let's get creative. Close your eyes and listen carefully to all the sounds around you. Describe them in the space below. You can use words or drawings to express yourself.

By now you should be a bit more relaxed. Focus on yourself and forget about the world out there. Breathe deeply.

Answer the following questions:

What is it that you want to do with your life?

What am I good at and what can I improve on?

What is my biggest fear?

Sestet (six-line poem):

Think of an object and write a poem about it.
Take the following rules into consideration:

- Line 1: Use at least one word describing the object.
- Line 2: Use at least two words describing the object.
- Line 3: Use at least three words describing the object.
- Line 4: Use at least four words describing the surroundings of the object.
- Line 5: Use a five-word sentence about the object.
- Line 6: Use just one word.

Aerobics

You will need:
- 1 sound system
- 1 laptop

Site:
- Preferably outdoor, but in case of bad weather an indoor area, which is large enough to accommodate the group, can also be used.

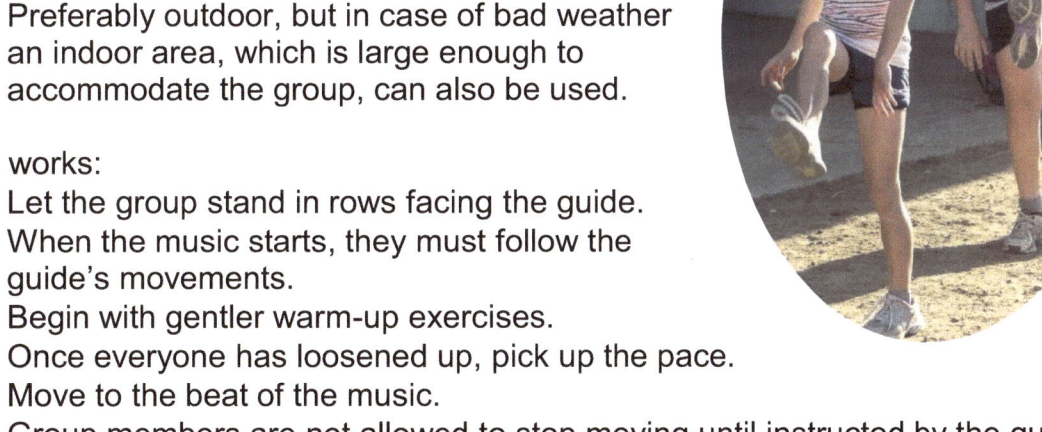

How it works:
- Let the group stand in rows facing the guide.
- When the music starts, they must follow the guide's movements.
- Begin with gentler warm-up exercises.
- Once everyone has loosened up, pick up the pace.
- Move to the beat of the music.
- Group members are not allowed to stop moving until instructed by the guide.
- The group must be careful not to kick or touch one another while moving.
- A few minutes before the music ends, have the group stretch out.

After the session:
- Pack up the sound equipment and laptop and store it in a safe place.

Morning Hike

Preparation:
- Make sure all the guides know the hiking route well.
- Wake up the group and give them 10 minutes to get ready.
- Instruct them to dress comfortably, with closed-toe shoes and hats.
- No pyjamas are allowed.
- Instruct the group members to each take a full water bottle with them.
- Make sure all the group members are wearing sunscreen.
- Find out if any of the group members have asthma and make sure they have their asthma pumps with them.
- Make sure at least one of the guides has a first aid kit with them.

How it works:
- While hiking, there must always be one guide in front and one guide at the back of the group.
- Make sure none of the group members are left behind along the way.
- The purpose of this activity is to enjoy nature. Guides can use the opportunity to tell the group more about the flora and fauna of the area.
- Solitaire is a great activity to add to a morning hike (see the instructions earlier in this section).

After the session:
- Make sure all the group members are accounted for.
- Ask them what they have learnt during the hike.
- Give them time to refill their water bottles.
- Tell them what the next activity is going to be and what time it will start.

Day Activities

Orienteering

You will need:
- 1 orienteering map per team (see the example following these instructions)
- 1 aerial photo of the site per team (if available)
- 1 laminated scoresheet per team (make laminated copies of the scoresheet following these instructions to reuse with future groups)
- 1 whiteboard marker per team
- 1 clipboard per team
- 1 watch for time-keeping
- 1 set of 10 reflector boards, each with a number from 1–10 and a letter from the word ATMOSPHERE on it (see the example following these instructions)

Note: standard orienteering boards are 200 x 200 mm red and white square boards.

Site:
- Any wide open field.

How it works:
- Hand each team an orienteering map, along with the rest of the equipment they will need.
- Optional: Give each team a rope with loops tied in it. Instruct the team members to hold onto a loop in the rope throughout the activity, so that the teams can't split up.
- Help the teams establish where north is.
- Indicate the base camp on the map.
- Give the teams a time to be back at base camp, then send them into the field.

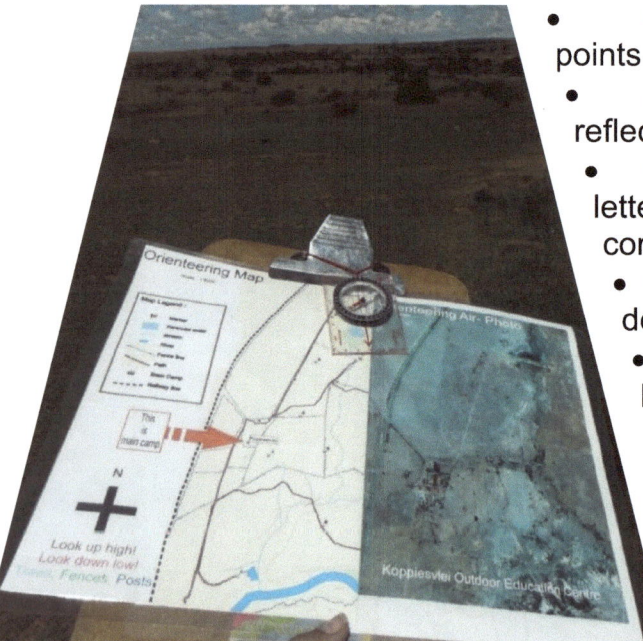

- Guides must place themselves at vantage points from where they will be able to see the teams.
- In the field, the teams must search for the 10 reflector boards using the orienteering map.
- On their scoresheet, each team must fill in the letter on each reflector board next to its corresponding number.
- Once a team has all the letters, they must decipher the word.
- A different amount of points are allocated per letter, as well as for deciphering the word.
- The team with the highest score wins.

Special rules:
- Teams do not need to find the reflector boards in order.
- Teams must stay on the marked paths at all times and must not try to find shortcuts – there aren't any.
- Teams may not split up at any time, as members may get lost without a map. Should a team split up, they will be disqualified.
- Teams may not pick up or harm any plant or animal in the field. Some animals are dangerous and some may be harmed if disturbed.
- Do not cross or go near any railway lines.
- Teams must close all gates that they pass through.
- Do not go near or cross any rivers or bridges.
- Remind teams that cows will not hurt them unless they are teased.
- Should a team member get hurt, two members must stay behind with the injured person while the rest of the team returns to base camp for help.
- Teams must be back at base camp at the time indicated by the guide.

After the session:
- Mark each team's scoresheet and calculate their score out of 2 000.
- Wipe the scoresheets clean.
- Collect all the equipment from the teams and put them away.
- Put any scrap paper in a recycling bin, if available.

Example of a reflector board:

ORIENTEERING ANSWERSHEET

NUMBER	LETTER	POINTS
1	A	75
2	E	300
3	E	350
4	H	50
5	M	50
6	O	75
7	P	125
8	R	100
9	S	125
10	T	250

DECIPHERING WORD: 500 points

Total score _____ *out of 2000*

ATMOSPHERE

Clue : It is all around us.

ORIENTEERING SCORESHEET

NUMBER	LETTER	POINTS
1		75
2		300
3		350
4		50
5		50
6		75
7		125
8		100
9		125
10		250

DECIPHERING WORD: 500 points

Total score _____ *out of 2000*

— — — — — — —

Clue : It is all around us.

Example of an orienteering map:

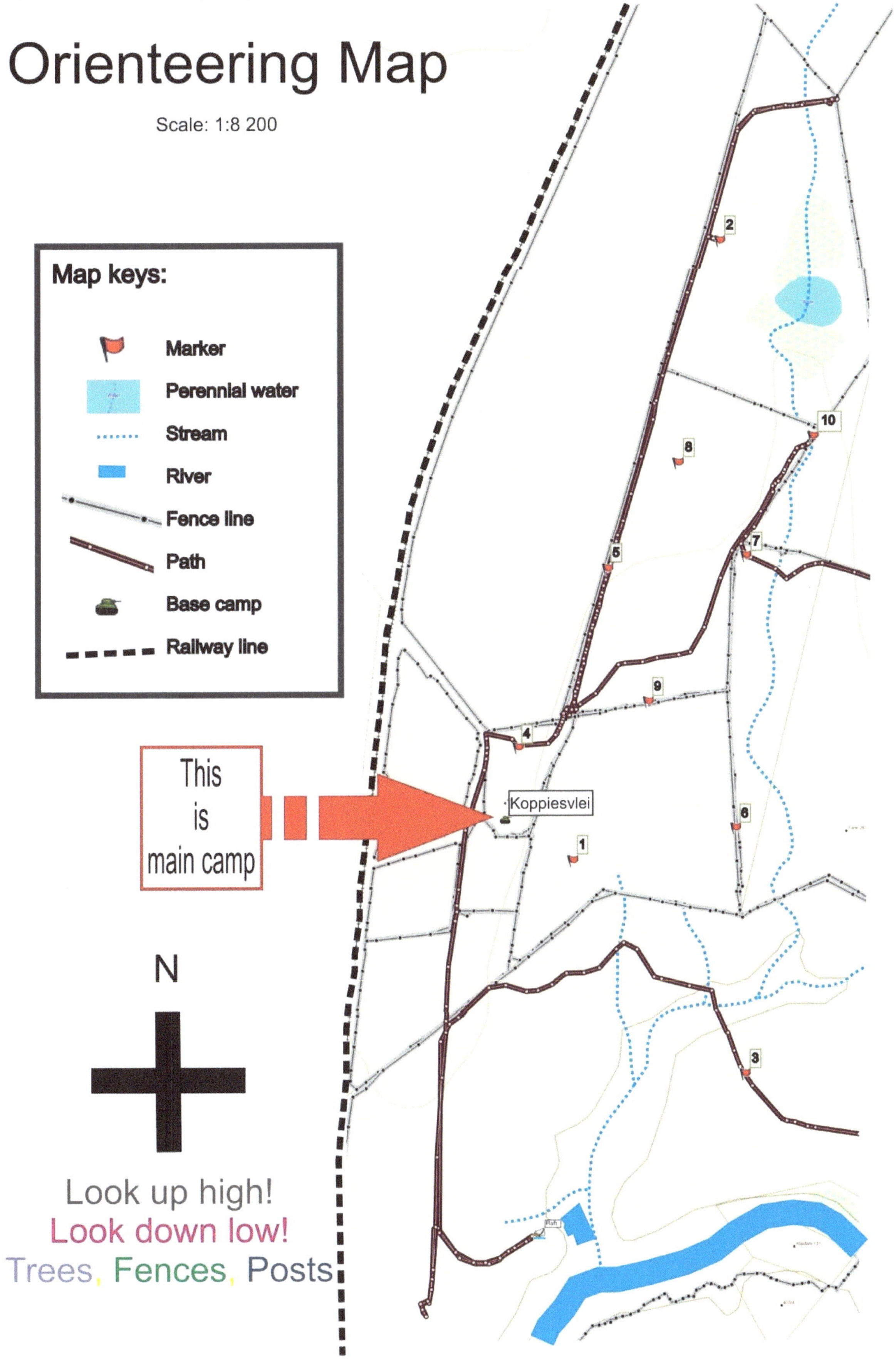

Orienteering Map
Scale: 1:8 200
Map keys:
Marker
Perennial water
Stream
River
Fence line
Path
Base camp
Railway line
This is main camp
Koppiesvlei
1
2
3
4
5
6
7
8
9
10
N
Look up high!
Look down low!
Trees, Fences, Posts

Adventure Race (Variation on Orienteering)

You will need:
- 5 x 5 l tubs, each containing:
    - 3 plastic cups
    - 3 ping pong balls
    - 1 pencil
    - Prestik (reusable adhesive)
    - 20 marbles
    - 8 metal nuts
    - 1 chopstick
    - 1 tin can
    - 48 bottle caps
    - 1 straw

- 5 x 5 l containers with water.
- 1 clipboard per team
- 1 whiteboard marker per team
- 1 race/orienteering map per team (see the example given for the previous activity)
- 1 race/orienteering scoresheet per team (make laminated copies of the scoresheet given for the previous activity)

Site:
- Any wide open field.

How it works:
- As per the original orienteering activity, teams need to find the reflector boards and complete their scoresheet.
- Along the way, teams will need to complete various timed challenges (see below).
  There are five challenges. Five staff members, each with a resource tub (see above) and water tub, will sit themselves down at every second marker.
- Teams get 30 minutes to complete each challenge. The time for the next challenge starts as soon as they leave the previous marker/challenge, so they must move fast.
- For each challenge, teams are awarded points for every team member who successfully completes that challenge, in addition to the normal orienteering points

Challenges:
LEVEL 1 – JUMPER
You will need:
- 3 plastic cups
- 3 ping pong balls
- 5 l water

How it works:
- Place the three cups in a row, 6 cm apart from each other.
- Fill each of the three cups to the brim with water.
- Hand the team member the three ping pong balls.
- Each team member gets three balls to blow from the first cup to the second cup to the third cup, without touching the ball.
- The team member places the first ping pong ball into the first cup and starts to blow. If the ball falls out of any of the cups, that ball is out of play and the team member continues with the remaining balls.
- Keep topping up the water in between team members so that the cups remain filled to the brim.
- Team members are awarded a full point if they can successfully blow the ball all the way to the third cup. If they only get as far as the second cup, half a point is awarded for the effort.

LEVEL 2 – MARBLE BOWLING
You will need:
- 1 pencil
- Prestik (reusable adhesive)
- 20 marbles

How it works:
- Stand the pencil upright on a rock, using the prestik.
- Each team member gets a chance to try and hit the pencil by throwing the marbles at it, one by one, from a distance of 1.5 m.
- Each time a team member hits the pencil with a marble, they are awarded two points.

LEVEL 3 – NUT STACK

You will need:
- 8 metal nuts
- 1 chopstick

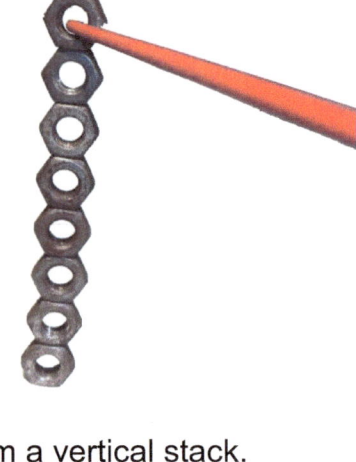

How it works:
- Make sure there is a level surface for the team to work on (use the tub lid).
- Each team member gets a chance to try and stack the eight metal nuts on top of each other, using only the chopstick.
- Using only one hand, slide all the metal nuts onto the chopstick.
- One by one, slide the nuts onto the flat surface to form a vertical stack.
- The stack must be freestanding for at least three seconds before collapsing for points to be awarded.
- Points are awarded as follows:
    - one point for four nuts stacked
    - two points for five nuts stacked
    - three points for eight nuts stacked

LEVEL 4 – POP TOP FLOP

You will need:
- 1 tin can
- 48 bottle caps

How it works:
- Place the tin can about 1.5 m away from the team.
- Each team member gets a chance to try and flip at least 10 of the 48 bottle caps into the tin can, using only their thumb.
- Points are awarded as follows:
    - two points for 5 caps
    - four points for 10 caps

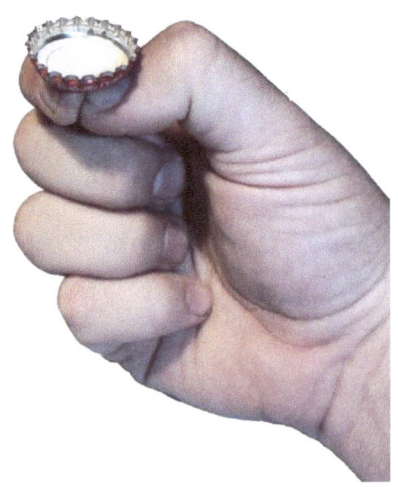

LEVEL 5 – LOLLIPOPPER

- 1 ping pong ball
- 3 metal nuts
- Prestik (reusable adhesive)
- 1 straw

How it works:

- Stand the straw upright on a flat surface (e.g. tub lid), using the prestik.
- Each team member gets a chance to balance the ping pong ball on top of the straw.
- Stack the three nuts, then balance the ping pong ball on top of it.
- Now pick up the stack and slide the nuts onto the straw until the ping pong ball is left balancing on top of the straw.
- Each team member who successfully completes this challenge is awarded five points.

Special rules:

- See the special rules for the original orienteering activity, plus the following additional rules:
- Teams must find the reflector boards in the order indicated on their scoresheets.
- Teams may not move on to the next reflector board until the guide has indicated that they may.
- The team with the highest score wins.

After the session:

- Tally the scores of each team.
- Make sure that every item that should be in each tub is there. If not, make a note of missing items.
- Collect all the equipment from the teams and put them away.

Archery

You will need (quantities will vary according to group size):
- Target buds
- Paper targets
- Target pins
- Bow stands
- Arrows
  - Checks:
    - Nocks attached and complete
    - Shafts straight
    - Points attached and fastened
    - Fletches attached and in good condition
- Recurve bows
  - Checks:
    - Poundage of the bows taken
    - Knocking points attached
    - Strings waxed
    - Arrow rests attached
- Wrist protectors
- Scoresheet on a clipboard with pencil
- Whistle

Site:
- A shooting range.

How it works:
- Explain the parts of the recurve bow to the group (see image).
- Explain the parts of the arrow to the group (see image).
- Show them how to load the arrow into the bow.
- Show them how to hold the bow and take aim.
- Tell them to aim first, then draw the bow and release.

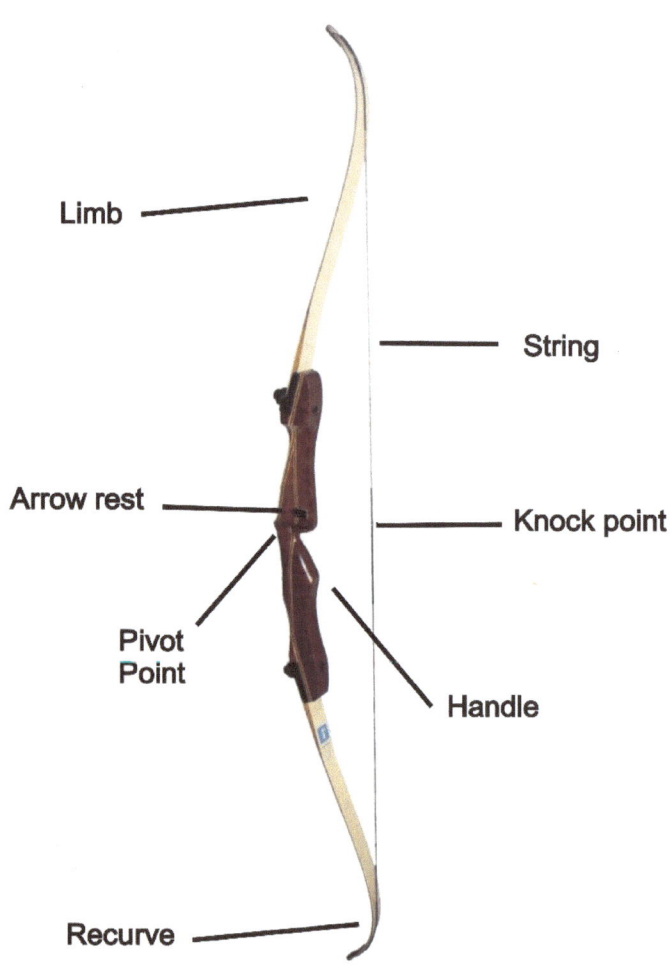

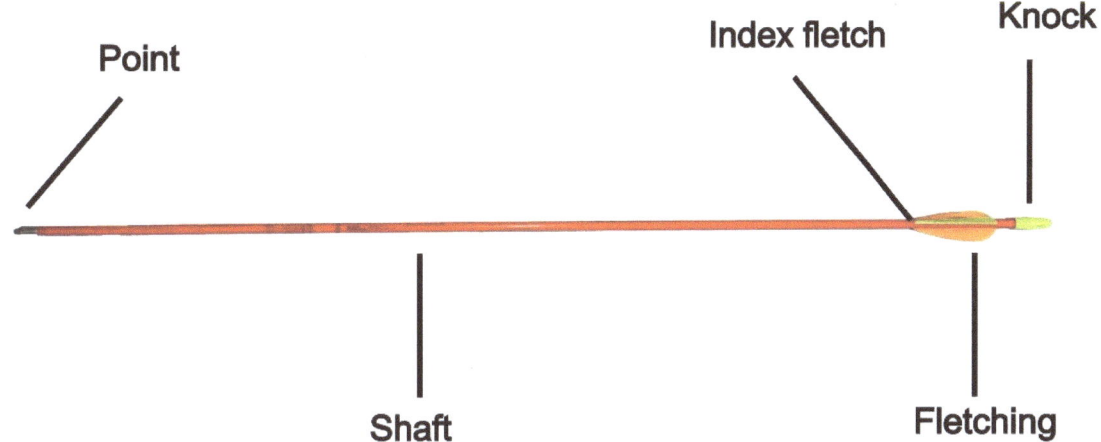

- Whistle 1 (short blow): Group members may come up to the shooting line, take the bow off the bow stand and place it on their toe.
- Whistle 2 (short blow): Participants may now load their first arrow, but may not shoot yet.
- Whistle 3 (long blow): If the shooting range is clear, the participants can now shoot all their arrows. When they are done, they must wait with the bow tip on their toe until all the participants have finished shooting.
- Whistle 4 (2 short blows): Participants may put their bows back on the stand and go fetch their arrows.
- Pick up all the arrows short of the target first. Next, pull out all the arrows that hit the target by their shafts (not fletches). Then go fetch the arrows that passed the target.
- Instruct the group that the ONLY way to carry their arrows is with the point towards the ground and the shaft resting on their shoulder.
- Group members must now put the arrows back in the stand and go take a seat.

Special rules:
- All group members must be seated when not shooting.
- Never point the weapon at anyone.
- Ensure that the shooting path is clear.
- NEVER shoot a dry shot (a shot without an arrow), as this will damage the bow.
- Never shoot at the ground or up into the air.
- Group members must treat the equipment in the proper way.
- Never distract the shooter or guide.
- Wear the necessary safety gear (Arm guard, closed shoes).
- Never shoot at animals (or guides!).
- If anyone wants to take a picture, they must ensure that they are not standing in the line of fire.

After the session:
- Check the equipment for any damage and repair it if necessary.
- Put all the equipment away.

Slingshot Shooting

You will need:
- 1 slingshot per person (check for damage to rubbers)
- 1 pair of safety goggles per person
- 1 bucket of small stones – 10 per person (the bullets)
- Tin cans in various sizes (the targets)

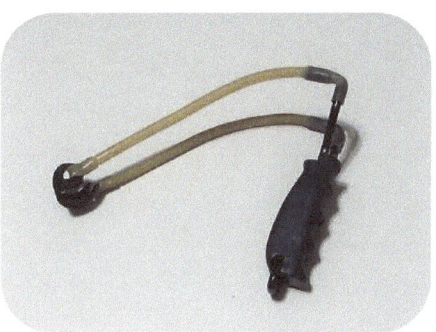

Site:
- A shooting range.

How it works:
- Show the group how a slingshot works.
- Pack the tin cans on a crossbar or other elevated area about 10 m from the group.
- Allocate a different amount of points to each tin can according to its size – with the smaller cans counting more points.
- Each group member gets 10 stones to shoot at the tin cans.
- They can choose their own stones from the bucket.
- The group member who scores the most points wins.

Special rules:
- All group members must wear protective eyewear.
- When a group member is done with their 10 shots, they must go sit down and give someone else a chance.
- Everyone must stay clear of the shooters.
- Do not shoot dry shots (A shot without a rock in the sling).
- Group members must follow the instructions at all times.
- Everyone who is not shooting must be seated.
- Never point the weapon at anyone.

- Ensure that the shooting path is clear.
- All participants must obey the instructions at all times.
- Never shoot at the ground or up into the air.
- All participants must treat the equipment in the proper way.
- Never distract the shooter or guide.
- Never shoot towards animals (or guides!).
- If anyone wants to take a picture, they must ensure that they are not standing in the line of fire.

After the session:
- Check the slingshots for damage and repair it if necessary.
- Put all the equipment away.

Blowguns

You will need:
- Dartboards or other painted targets (one per team)
- 5 darts per person, plus extra
- 3 blowguns
- 1 whistle
- 1 scoresheet on a clipboard with pencil

Site:
- Any safe, spacious indoor area.

How it works:
- Explain the rules very carefully (see "Special rules").
- Explain the basic parts of the blowgun to the group (see image).
- Explain the parts of the dart to the group (see image).

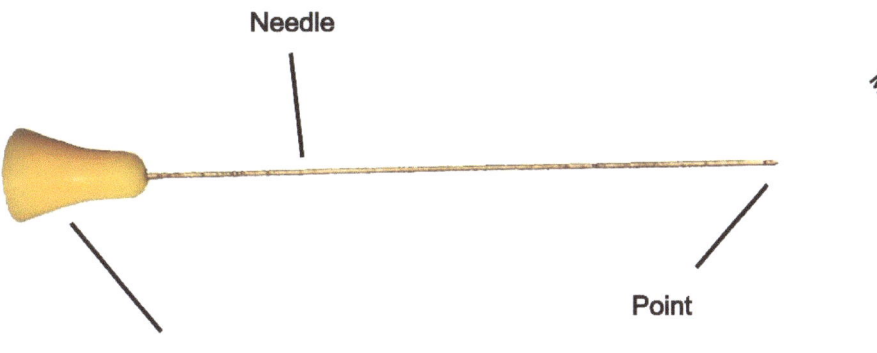

- Tell them that the blowgun and dart are not toys and can actually kill someone; therefore they should be very careful and follow the instructions at all times.
- Show the group how to load the dart into the blowgun: Only lightly drop the dart into the shaft. DO NOT PUSH THE DART INTO THE SHAFT!
- Show the group how to use the blowgun: Inhale before you put your mouth against the mouthpiece and then blow. DO NOT INHALE WITH YOUR MOUTH AGAINST THE MOUTHPIECE, AS YOU WILL SUCK THE DART INTO YOUR MOUTH!
- Whistle 1 (short blow): Participants may come up to the shooting line three at a time and each pick up a blowgun.
- Whistle 2 (short blow): Participants may now load their first dart, but may not shoot yet.

- Whistle 3 (long blow): Participants may now shoot all their darts at the target. When they are done, they must put the blowgun down and go sit down until everyone has had a turn.
- Whistle 4 (2 short blows): All participants may go sit down while the guide fetches all the darts and tallies the scores. (Pull the darts out by their needles, not by their fletches.)
- Scoring works as follows:
    - Inner bull = 50 points
    - Outer bull = 25 points
    - Double ring = double the segment number
    - Triple ring = triple the segment number
    - Single score = the segment number as is
- After tallying the scores, the guide must place the darts back in the dart holder and whistle for the next shooters.

Special rules:
- Everyone who is not shooting must be seated.
- Never point the weapon at anyone.
- Ensure that the shooting path is clear.
- All participants must obey the instructions at all times.
- Never shoot at the ground or up into the air.
- All participants must treat the equipment in the proper way.
- Never distract the shooter or guide.
- Never shoot towards animals (or guides!).
- If anyone wants to take a picture, they must ensure that they are not standing in the line of fire.

After the session:
- Check the equipment for damage and repair if necessary.
- Put all the equipment away.

Capture the Flag

You will need:
- 1 bucket filled with 1 l paint per team per round (different colour for each team)
  - To make paint: Mix 3 cups of flour with 4 cups of water until all the lumps are dissolved, then add a drop of food colouring.
  - The above recipe makes about 1.5 l.
  - Place any extra paint in the fridge.
- 1 bucket and sponge per team (for washing)
- 25 l of water (for washing)
- 1 x 5 ml syringe (without needle) per team member, plus extras
- 1 big flag per team, matching the team's colour
- 8 small flags per team, matching the team's colour
- 1 bandanna per team member, matching the team's colour
- 1 whistle

Site:
- A bushy area with enough strategic hiding places for flags and one home base per team.
- Make sure the site is not too rocky.

How it works:
- The object of the game is to retrieve as many of the opposition's flags as possible from the playing field without getting shot with paint.
- Divide the group into two teams.
- Show each team their home base and the boundaries of their territory.
- After explaining the game, hand each team member a bandanna and a syringe.
- Take each team to their home base where their bucket of paint, as well as the sponges and water for washing, will be waiting.
- Teams can fill the syringes with paint and use them as weapons to shoot the opposition with.
- Give the teams time to strategise while you hide the flags.
- Put the big flags at the furthest ends of the playing field, and put the smaller flags in visible but strategic places throughout each team's territory.
- Once the flags have been hidden, give one short blow on the whistle to start the game.

- A team will receive points for every flag that they return to their home base:
  - Big flag = 50 points
  - Small flags = 10 points each
- The game ends when one team has retrieved all the other teams' flags.
- Give one long blow on the whistle to indicate the end of the game.

- If there is time for another round, swop the two teams' territories.

Special rules:
- If a participant gets shot, they have to return to their team's home base and wash off all the paint before continuing to play. If they play while being shot, they will be disqualified.
- If a participant gets shot while carrying one of the opposition's flags, they must stand still with the flag in their hand until someone from their team takes the flag from them.
- Teams are not allowed to move any of their own flags. If a participant is caught with their own team's flag in hand, the points for that flag will automatically go to the other team.
- While a participant is filling their syringe at their home base, they have immunity and may not be shot within a 2 m range of their home base. The same rule applies when participants are washing the paint off themselves. Furthermore, participants who have immunity are not allowed to shoot anyone.

After the session:
- Collect and wash all the equipment immediately after the game.
- The two parts of each syringe must be pulled apart before being stored to prolong its life.
- Apply petroleum jelly to the rubbers of the syringes.
- Repair any damage to the equipment.
- Put all the equipment away.

Bridge Building

You will need:
- 6 x 1.5 m wooden poles per team
- 1 set of ropes per team (1 x 5 m; 1 x 10 m; 1 x 15 m)

Site:
- Designated site for bridge building where a 2 m wide trench has been dug out.

How it works:
- Explain to the teams that they are stuck on one side of a river (the trench) and need to build a bridge so that their whole team can get to the other side.
- The teams must use their poles and ropes to build the bridge.
- Once a team's bridge is complete, the guide must test it to make sure it is stable and safe to cross.
- If the guide is satisfied with the bridge, the team may cross over to the other side one by one.
- The teams need to get all their equipment (used and unused) to the other side as well.
- The first team to get all their members and equipment to the other side wins.

Special rules:
- The teams can build their bridges any way they want.
- Teams may only cross to the other side using the bridge.
- The bridge is not allowed to touch the inside of the trench, only the sides.

After the session:
- The participants must untie all the ropes and neatly fold them.
- If necessary, wash the ropes (without detergent).
- Put the ropes away.
- Place the poles to one side of the trench, ready to be used by the next group.
- If the poles are not going to be used for some time, store them in a safe, dry place.

Raft Building

You will need:
- About 6 wooden planks per team (+/- 2 m long)
- About 12 x 20 l plastic drums per team
- 3 x 10 m rope per team
- 2 life jackets per team

Site:
- A dam or lake that is deep enough for the rafts to float, but shallow enough for a safe crossing.

How it works:
- The objective is to build a raft sturdy enough to transport two people to the other side of the dam and back.
- Each team may use as many of the drums and planks they have received as they see fit.
- Teams may start building their rafts right away.
- When they are done, they need to call the guide for inspection.
- First, the guide must test the raft on dry land to make sure it is stable.
- Next, the team must move their raft into the water and the guide must test the stability once more.
- Once the guide is satisfied, the team members may get onto the raft two at a time and start crossing the dam.
- The first team to get all their members across the river and back wins.
- Optionally, teams could also be instructed to fetch something from the other side of the dam and bring it back with them.

Special rules:
- Team members must put on life jackets before getting on the raft.
- The rest of the team is allowed to assist the raft into the water up to knee-depth.
- The whole raft must return; no piece may be left behind at the other side of the dam.

After the session:
- Let the team members disassemble their rafts.
- Make sure that there are no knots in the ropes.
- Rinse any excess mud off all the equipment and put all the equipment away neatly.
- Tie all the drums together and fasten them to a tree so that they can't float away.
- Make sure the area is left behind clean.

Survival Game

Note: The Survival Game can also be combined with raft building.

You will need:
- 1 egg per team
- 1 tea bag per team
- 1 large tin per team
- 2 matches per team
- 1 matchbox per team
- 1 magnifying glass per team
- 20 l plastic drums of water for extinguishing fires
    - A crate containing all of the above must be prepared for each team and taken to the survival site beforehand.
- 1 flat rock per team
- Enough firewood per team (placed at the survival site beforehand)

Site:
- Any site with a "survivor" feel to it.

How it works:
- Give each team all their equipment and show them their designated fireplaces.
- Make sure the wind is not blowing so that there is no chance of a bush fire.
- Each team must start a fire to make hot tea and cook their egg.
- If they don't manage to get a fire going with their two matches, the team must find another way to light it, e.g. the magnifying glass.
- Each team must keep their drum of water close in case the fire needs to be put out.

Special rules:
- The egg is not allowed to be cooked in the tea.
- Fires must NOT be left unattended.
- Fires may only be made in the designated fireplaces as allocated by the guide.
- No horseplay is allowed around the fire.

Potential outcomes of the game:
- The children are likely to cook water for tea in the tin.
- Some children might try to cook the egg on the rock; others might bury the egg and make a fire on top of the soil to cook the egg in its shell.

Do not give them too many clues or ideas; let them come up with solutions.

After the session:
- See the storage instructions for the raft-building equipment under the previous activity.
- Rinse out the tins and put them back in the crates, along with the rest of the equipment.
- Put the crates away.
- Ensure that the area is left behind clean.

Wall Climbing

Note: This activity can only be performed at campsites where a climbing wall is installed.
Ensure that you have the required training in your country before presenting this activity.

There should always be a rope on the climbing wall. Either a 2 mm accessory cord (P-cord) or the 10.5 mm climbing rope.

You will need:
- Wall climbing rope
    - Use a 2 mm accessory cord (P-cord) and 10.5 mm climbing rope.
- Belay device (e.g. a Petzl GRI-GRI) with the correct carabiner
- Waist harnesses for climbers
- Harness for belayer/guide
- 1 belay carabiner (belay master)
- Anchor rope with 3 oval steel carabiners

Setting up the climbing rope:
- Untie the P-cord and tie the end closest to you (not closest to the wall) to the climbing rope with two fisherman's knots. Make the one knot as close to the tip of the rope as possible.
- Pull on the accessory cord, which will pull the climbing rope up into position.
- Tie a figure 8 with a loop knot at the end of the cord closest to the wall.
- Hook the belay master into the loop.
- Assemble the belay device in place on the other end of the rope.
- Hook an offset D carabiner into the belay device.

Site:
- Designated climbing wall.

How it works:
- Start by explaining the activity and rules to the group (see "Special rules").
- Demonstrate how to correctly put on a harness.
- Hook the belay device into your harness.
- Call the first climber to the wall.
- Make sure that the climber's harness is tightened correctly.
- Hook the climber to the rope with the belay carabiner and fasten the carabiner.
- Take a comfortable position and get ready to belay. Instruct the climber to wait for you to get into place before climbing.
- Once you are ready, tell the climber to start climbing.
- Encourage and help your climber as far as possible.
- When they have reached the top of the wall, ask them to descend by holding onto the rope while kicking themselves away from the wall.
- Let them descend at an even pace, keeping the brake ready at all times.

- When the climber is back on the ground, help them unhook the rope.
- Call the next climber.

Special rules:
- Ensure the safety of the climbers at all times.
- Do not step on the rope, as this could damage it.
- Group members may not fiddle with any of the equipment.
- No one may stand at the bottom of the climbing wall, except the climber and the guide.
- No one may stand behind the belayer/guide.
- Group members must follow the guide's instructions at all times.

After the session:

- Place all the equipment in its designated storage space and leave the climbing wall as you found it.

Create a Country (Cardboard Flags)

You will need:
- 1 explanation sheet per team (make laminated copies of the explanation sheet following these instructions)
- 1 x A3 sheet of cardboard per team
- 1 pencil per team
- 1 tin with colouring pencils and crayons per team
- 2 x A4 sheets of scrap paper per team

Site:
- Indoor area.

How it works:
- Each team must create their own country, using the explanation sheet as a guideline.
- The teams can use the pencils, crayons and cardboard to create their flag. They can work out their language and write their anthem on the scrap paper.
- Give the teams ample time to conceptualise their country's symbols and to practise their anthem before singing it to the rest of the group.
- During the rest of the camp, each team's anthem will be sung before the start of every activity.

Special rules:
- Teams may not use existing countries.
- Each country's language should be a completely new language that the team made up themselves.
- The anthem can be written and performed in any existing language.

After the session:
- Collect all the equipment and put it away.
- Put all the scrap paper in a recycling bin, if available.
- Create bunting with the teams' flags and put it up in the main hall.

Variation: Create a Country (Material Flags)

You will need:
- 1 explanation sheet per team (make laminated copies of the explanation sheet following these instructions)
- 1 x A3 piece of fabric per team
- 1 pencil per team
- 1 tin with colouring pencils and crayons per team
- 2 x A4 sheets of scrap paper per team
- Enough paintbrushes per team
- Enough fabric paint per team
- A piece of cardboard for each team to press on while painting the flag
- 1 tin of water per team (for washing paintbrushes)

Site:
- Use an indoor area for planning and an outdoor area for painting.

How it works:
- See "Create a Country (Cardboard Flags)".
- Instead of drawing the flags on cardboard, teams must paint their flags on fabric.

Special rules:
- Team members may not paint one another or any surfaces or furniture in the area.

After the session:
- Wash the brushes and any other equipment that has paint on it.
- Collect all the equipment and put it away.
- Put all the scrap paper in a recycling bin, if available.
- Create bunting with the teams' flags and put it up in the main hall.

Create a Bumper Sticker

You will need:
- 1 explanation sheet per team (make laminated copies of the explanation sheet following these instructions)
- 1 x A3 piece of fabric per team
- 1 pencil per team
- 1 tin with colouring pencils and crayons per team
- 2 x A4 sheets of scrap paper per team
- Enough paintbrushes per team
- Enough fabric paint per team
- A piece of cardboard for each team to press on while painting the flag
- 1 tin of water per team (for washing paintbrushes)

Site:
- Use an indoor area for planning and an outdoor area for painting.

How it works:
- Each team has to design a bumper sticker on their piece of fabric.
- The theme of the bumper sticker should be either leadership or respect, depending on which one the guide chooses.
- See the explanation sheet for further instructions.

Special rules:
- Team members may not paint one another or any surfaces or furniture in the area.

After the session:
- Wash the brushes and any other equipment that has paint on it.
- Collect all the equipment and put it away.
- Put all the scrap paper in a recycling bin, if available.
- Create bunting with the teams' stickers and put it up in the main hall.

Create Your Own Country
- Where in the world would your country be?
- What is the name of your country?
- Create a flag for your country.
- Create a language for your country. Write and present one sentence.
- What will the national food be?
- Write a national anthem for your new country and perform it.

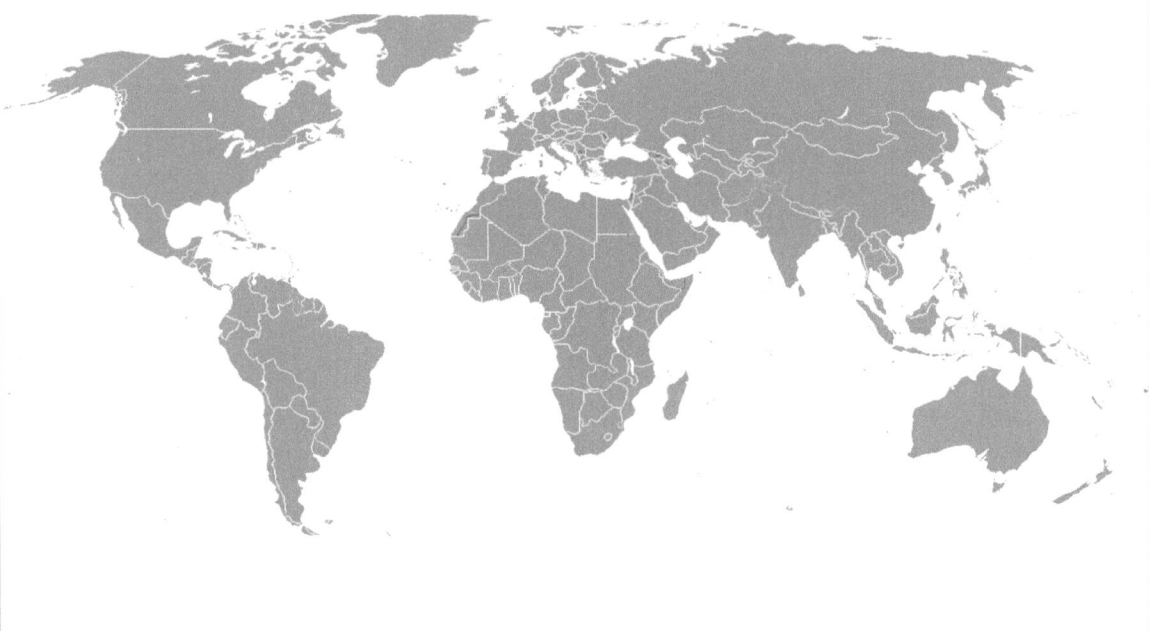

Design a Bumper Sticker About Respect
Design a bumper sticker that includes the following:
- The word "respect"
- A slogan about why respect is important

Design a Bumper Sticker About Leadership
Design a bumper sticker that includes the following:
- The word "leadership"
- A slogan about why leadership is important

Obstacle Course

Preparation:
- Make sure that each element on the obstacle course is safe for use (e.g. check that all bolts are fastened and that there is no wear and tear that could cause injuries).
- Make sure that the whole area is clear of any hazardous items such as glass, loose rocks, etc.

Site:
- Designated obstacle course.

How it works:
- Explain the rules of the obstacle course to the group.
- Divide the group into teams of two.
- The two team members must take turns to complete the obstacle course, with the other team member supporting them.
- If one of the teams has an odd number of people, that team must start first.
- Guides must pay close attention to all the participants.
- Start at the beginning of the obstacle course and explain each of the elements separately: Here are some elements that participants may encounter in an obstacle course:
    - Stepping tyres: Cross over from one end to the other by stepping from one embedded tyre to the next. Do not skip any tyres.

    - Swinging balance beam: Cross over from one end to the other without falling off.

- Pole balance: Holding onto the rope with one hand, balance on the pole between the two embedded tyres.

- Swing: Swing from the one tyre platform to the other.

- TP shuffle: Balance on the cable and walk from one end to the other.

- Tyre swing: Place your feet on the brim of the tyre, NOT on top. Take care not to get pinched by the cable when sitting on top of the tyre. Be careful not to place your feet inside the rim-cavity of the tyre, as this may cause an ankle injury if you fall and your foot gets stuck. Swing from one tyre to the other.

- Crocodile walk: Cross over from one end to the other by holding onto the top rope and shuffling your feet along the bottom rope.

- X-cross bridge: Hold onto the top rope with your hands, and shuffle your feet along the bottom rope. When you get to the X, cross over so that your feet remain at the bottom and your hands on top.

- Stepping logs: Cross over from one end to the other by stepping from one log to the next. Do not skip any logs.

- Monkey ropes: Cross over from one end to the other by swinging from one monkey rope to the next. Do not skip any ropes.

- Balance beam: Cross over from one end to the other without falling off. Do not crawl, as you could get splinters under your skin.

- Cookie press: Crawl through (NOT over) the tyres from one end to the other.

- Cargo net: Climb over the cargo net from one side to the other.

- Triple see-saw: Cross over each see-saw and climb over the tyre obstacle to the next see-saw extension.

- Tyre bridge: Cross over from one end to the other without falling off.

- Wobbly bridge: Cross over from one end to the other without falling off.

Special rules:
- Safety comes first!
- Once they have started the obstacle course, participants are no longer allowed to touch the ground.
- If a participant should fall off an obstacle or touch the ground at any time while completing the course, they have to redo the specific obstacle they were busy completing before continuing.
- Only one participant at a time is allowed on an obstacle.

After the session:
- Ask the group members to describe their experience of the obstacle course.
- Make sure that the area is left behind clean.
- Report any damage of the obstacle course.

Variation on Obstacle Course

How it works:
- See instructions for the original obstacle course.
- The obstacle course can also be completed by larger teams with a "baby" (a 10 l tub or bucket filled with water). They must get the "baby" through the entire obstacle course while spilling as little water as possible.
- Only one team member is allowed to carry the bucket through each obstacle. Team members can alternate between obstacles.
- The rest of the team may offer support, but may not touch the bucket.
- Once all the teams have completed the course, measure (or weigh) the water left in each team's bucket to determine the winner.
- The obstacle course can also be completed in timed laps. The team with the best time wins.

Problem Course

Preparation:
- Make sure that each element on the problem course is safe for use (e.g. check that all bolts are fastened and that there is no wear and tear that could cause injuries).
- Make sure that the whole area is clear of any hazardous items like glass, loose rocks, etc.

Site:
- Designated problem course.

How it works:
- Divide the group into teams.
- Here are some elements that participants may encounter in a problem course:

    o Mock "electric" fence:
        - Make sure the fence is set at the right height for the age group.
        - Tell the teams that they are stuck in a lion camp. The whole team must cross over the "electric" fence in order to avoid getting eaten.
        - Each team has 10 minutes to cross over the fence one by one.
        - They should help one another.
        - No one may crawl underneath the fence or pass around the sides.
        - No one is allowed to touch the fence or wooden posts, not even with their clothing.
        - If a team member touches the fence, the team has to start over.

- Spider's web:
  - Tell the teams that they are stuck on a deserted planet. There is a spider's web through which the whole team must pass to get back to earth.
  - Each team gets 10 minutes to pass through the web.
  - No one is allowed to pass under, over or around the sides.
  - No one is allowed to touch the sides or the rope at any time.
  - Once someone has passed through a hole, that hole closes.
  - If a team member touches the sides or rope, the whole team has to start over and the holes that have already been used stay closed.

- Porthole:
  - Tell the teams that they are on a cruise ship that is sinking. Their whole team must pass through the porthole window onto the deck and into the lifeboat to avoid drowning. Only team members on the cruise ship can help those passing through the port window onto the deck.
  - Only team members on the lifeboat can help those getting down from the deck onto the lifeboat.

- Tyre bongle:
    - Each team must rebuild the tyre pyramid as it was found on one of the other poles provided.
    - Teams can only move one tyre at a time.
    - Only smaller tyres may be placed on bigger tyres.
    - The whole team must hold onto the tyre that is being moved.
    - Use only three poles for older groups.

- Speedy nitro swing:
    - Tell the teams that they are stuck on a riverbank. The river is going to flood and the only way to get to safety is on the "raft".
    - Each team has 10 minutes to get onto the "raft".
    - The whole team must get onto the "raft" by using the rope swing provided.
    - Team members are not allowed to touch the ground at any time. If a team member does, the whole team has to start over.
    - Swing from the starting point as indicated.
    - Once the whole team is on the "raft" they are safe and now need to get safely off the "raft".

- Lollipop stick:
    - Each team must get the tyre off the pole, touch the ground and put it back over the pole again.
    - The tyre is not allowed to touch the pole.
    - If the tyre touches the pole, the team must start over.
    - To avoid injury, the tyre may not be thrown.

- Lava island:
    - Tell the teams that they are stuck on a big island surrounded by lava.
    - Each team must get from the one big island on the one side to the other big island on the other side via the small islands in-between the two big islands.
    - Each team has two wooden planks and a brick to help them get across.
    - The brick is the only piece of equipment that may touch the ground/lava.
    - The wooden planks may only touch the islands and the brick, not the ground/lava.
    - Teams may not skip any of the small islands.
    - The whole team must get to the other side with all their equipment.

After the session:
- After each activity, sum up what happened. Discuss the following: What worked and why? What did each team do right and wrong? Did the whole team work together?
- Report any damaged equipment.

Group Dynamics

Please see the third book in the *Outdoor Education Resource Series* for a detailed discussion on group dynamics and activities relating to it.

Paintball

You will need:
- 4 corner flags (red)
- 1 paintball marker/gun per person
  Each gun should have a bullet hopper and gas cylinder.
- 1 paintball mask per person
- Enough paintballs per person
- Extra O-rings for gas bottles
- 1 key for gun adjustment
- 1 mask per referee
- 1 bib per referee
- 1 whistle

Site:
- Similar to the area where "Capture the flag" is played.

How it works:
- Divide the group into two teams.
- Take a walk around the field and clearly indicate the boundaries to everyone playing.
- Indicate the dead zone and make sure everyone knows not to shoot near or in it.
- Establish a time limit.
- Explain the rules of the game (see the variations below).
- Explain the safety rules and make sure that everyone understands them.
- Hand out the masks. All players must put on their masks before receiving a paintball gun. This is done in the dead zone.
- Once all the players have their masks on, they may receive their paintball guns and paintballs.
- Each team is then sent to their respective bases.
- Once the teams are ready, blow the whistle to start the game.
- The following are various ways to play paintball:

- VIP:
    - Each team must elect a VIP.
    - Teams may not know who the other team's VIP is.
    - Each team's goal is to protect their VIP while attempting to eliminate the opposing team's VIP.
    - All the general rules of paintball apply.
    - As soon as a team member is hit by a paintball, they are out of the game.
    - The VIP may also play with a gun, but it is often more exciting for the VIP to be unarmed.
    - A team wins once they eliminate the other team's VIP.
- Capture the flag:
    - See the instructions for "Capture the flag" earlier in this section.

Special rules:
- A player is hit if a paintball leaves a solid, coin-sized mark anywhere on the player's body or equipment.
- If they are unsure whether they have been hit, players can call for a paint check. The closest player to them will then come and check them for paint.
- Once a player is hit, they must raise their gun over their head, shout that they are hit and quickly move into the dead zone.
- Once one of the teams has completed the objective, all the players on the field must be notified.
- AT NO POINT DURING THE GAME MAY PLAYERS REMOVE THEIR MASKS. ONLY ONCE THEY HAVE HANDED IN THEIR GUNS AND ARE SAFELY IN THE DEAD ZONE MAY THEY REMOVE THEIR MASKS.

Safety rules:
- Players must wear their masks at all times – there are no exceptions to this rule.
- Do not drink and play.
- No blind firing is allowed – players may not fire if they can't see what they are firing at.
- Because close-range shots are very painful, it is customary to give opponents within 5 metres of you the chance to surrender. Once they have surrendered, players are out of the game.

After the session:
- Clean all the equipment and put it away.

Traditional Games

You will need (quantities will vary according to group size):
- Rope
- Hessian bags
- Bag of dried corn kernels
- Eggs
- Tablespoons
- Packet of toffees
- Apples
- Cake flour
- 3 large basins
- 4 small basins
- 10 x 500 ml plastic bottles filled with cooldrink
- 10 nursing teats
- Rusks
- 1 whistle

Site:
- Any wide outdoor space.

How it works:
- Divide the group into equal teams.
- Complete each activity as follows:

    o Three-legged race:
    - Two members of each team must pair up and tie their inside legs together.
    - They have to run to the other side of the playing field and back.
    - Now the next two members of each team must go.
    - The first team to finish gets a point.

    o Bag race:
    - Each team gets a hessian bag.
    - One person from each team must climb inside their bag and run or bounce as fast as they can to the other side of the playing field and back.
    - As soon as one member returns, the next one may start.
    - The first team to finish gets a point.

- Corn spit:
    - Each team member gets a corn kernel which they must spit as far as possible.
    - The person whose corn kernel lands the farthest away gets a point for their team.

- Egg throw:
    - Each team stands in a circle, about an arm's length apart.
    - The teams must now throw the egg from one person to the next and take a step back every time the egg completes a circle.
    - The group whose egg breaks last gets a point.

- Egg throw – variation:
    - Two team members stand opposite each other and throw the egg to each other.
    - After every throw, both team members must take a step back before throwing the egg again.
    - The team whose egg breaks last gets a point.

- Egg-on-spoon team run:
    - Divide each team in two and let the two halves stand at opposite ends of the field.
    - The starting side of each team gets two spoons while the opposite side gets only one.
    - One team member must run from the starting side to the opposite side with an egg on a spoon.
    - Once the team member reaches the other side, they must transfer the egg to another spoon, held by another team member, without touching the egg.
    - The next team member must now take the egg back to the starting side, and the sequence continues until all team members have had a turn.
    - Team members who have had a turn must sit down.
    - The first team to complete the challenge gets a point.
    - If a team's egg falls and breaks, that team is eliminated.

- Egg-on-spoon run:
    - One member of each team stands at the starting line with an egg on a spoon.
    - When the whistle blows, they have to race to the finish line without touching or breaking their eggs.
    - The first person to cross the finish line wins their group a point.

- Apple and toffee hunt:
    - Fill the large basins halfway with water. Cut the apples into slices and throw them in the water.
    - Fill the small basins halfway with cake flour and strategically hide the toffees in the flour.
    - Each team member gets a turn to fish an apple slice from one of the large basins, using only their mouths and with their hands behind their backs.
    - Once a team member has caught an apple slice, they must chew and swallow or spit it out, move on to one of the small basins and search for a toffee using only their mouth.
    - Once they have found a toffee, the next team member may go.
    - Team members who have had a turn must sit down.
    - The first team to finish gets a point.

- o Cooldrink challenge:
    - Place a nursing teat over each of the 500 ml bottles of cooldrink.
    - Each team must nominate two members to complete the challenge.
    - One team member must stand on their knees with their hands behind their back.
    - The other team member must hold the cooldrink bottle for the kneeling team member to drink from.
    - The first team to finish their cooldrink wins a point.

- o Rusk challenge:
    - One team member from each group must eat a rusk.
    - The first person to finish their rusk and blow the whistle wins their team a point.

Special rules:
- Everyone in the team must get a turn to complete each activity (except for the rusk challenge).
- No one is allowed to walk around or leave the site without permission.
- Teams must stay together.
- In the end, the team with the most points wins.

After the session:
- The winning team gets to go and wash their faces and clean up first.
- Pack up all the equipment and put it away.

Evening Activities

Goofy Olympics

You will need:
- Stand and scoresheet (make laminated copies of the scoresheet following these instructions)
- 4 orange cones
- 1 packet of sparklers
- 1 box of matches (to light sparklers)
- 1 sponge per team
- 1 x A4 sheet of scrap paper per team
- 1 stopwatch
- 1 plastic bowling set with 10 pins
- 1 tablespoon per team
- 1 pudding bowl per team
- 1 thumb wrestling ring
- 1 table
- 2 chairs
- 1 wooden number per team (use a different number for each team)

Site:
- Any suitable indoor space.

How it works:
- Divide the group into teams.
- Show the teams the scoresheet with the list of activities, and explain how many people need to compete in each activity.
- Give the teams three minutes to decide who will do which activities.
- Put two orange cones on either side of the playing area to indicate the start and finish lines.
- Light the sparklers to symbolise the Olympic torch.
- Let the participants in the first activity step forward.
- Explain each activity right before it commences.

  o Shot-put sponge:
    - Call the first team's participant to the start line and give them a sponge.
    - The participant must throw their sponge shot-put style as if it is very heavy.
    - If they throw the sponge normally, they will be disqualified.
    - Mark the landing position of the sponge with the corresponding team's wooden number.
    - Now call the next team's participant to the start line and let them throw their sponge.
    - Once all the teams have had a chance, determine who threw their sponge the furthest.
    - Award points for first to tenth place, e.g. 10 points for first place, nine points for second place, eight points for third place, etc.

- Disqualified teams get zero points.

- Javelin jet:
  - Call the first team's participants to the start line and let them stand one in front of the other.
  - The front participant gets an A4 sheet of scrap paper, which they have to fold into a jet in 10 seconds. They may not crumple the paper up or roll it into a ball.
  - When the guide says stop, the paper jet must be placed on the ground. The other participant may not alter the jet and must use it as is.
  - The other participant then steps forward and throws the jet, javelin-style, as far as they can.
  - Mark the position of the jet with the corresponding team's number.
  - Now call the next team's participants to the start line and let them throw their jet.
  - Once all the teams have had a chance, determine who threw their jet the furthest.
  - Award points for first to tenth place.

- 100 m sprint:
  - Call the first team's participant to the start line.
  - Let the participant run in one spot for what they estimate to be 10 seconds while timing them on the stopwatch.
  - Non-participating team members may not make any noise or tell the runner when to stop.
  - Write down the participant's actual time, as per the stopwatch. Note the time in seconds and milliseconds.
  - Now call the next team's participant to the start line and let them run.
  - Determine who is closest to 10 seconds.
  - Award points for first to tenth place, according to who is closest to 10 seconds.

- Leapfrog hurdles:
  - Call the participants of each team to the start line.
  - When the whistle blows, each team must leapfrog over each other all the way to the finish line and back.
  - The first team to cross the start line upon their return wins.
  - To win, both participants need to cross the line
  - Award points for first to tenth place.

- Plastic bowling
  - Stack the bowling pins as shown in the image.
  - Call the first team's participant to the start line.
  - Standing with their back to the bowling pins, the participant must roll the ball at the bowling pins from between their legs.
  - The participant gets three tries to knock over as many pins as possible.
  - One point is awarded for each pin that is knocked over.
  - Now call the next team's participant to the start line to bowl.
  - Award points for first to tenth place, according to who scored the most points on their best try.

- Wheelbarrow bike race:
  - Call the participants of each team to the start line. Let each pair stand one in front of the other.
  - The front participants must put their hands on the ground, while their team members grab their legs and pick them up in the air.
  - The front participants are now wheelbarrows, and their team members must push them all the way to the finish line and back.
  - The first team to cross the start line upon their return wins.
  - Award points for first to tenth place.
  - If you have limited space, let the teams compete one at a time in timed laps. Award points for first to tenth place, according to who completed the activity in the shortest time.

- Pudding bowl swimming race:
  - Call the participants of each team to the start line. Let each pair stand facing each other.
  - Hand one participant from each team a spoon and the other a bowl filled with water (the pool).
  - The participants holding the pool must hold it at chest height.
  - Without touching the bowl or spilling any water, the participants holding the spoons must spoon water out of the pool and feed it to their team members.
  - The first team to finish their water must sit down.
  - Blow the whistle to indicate that all the teams must stop and sit down with their pool between them.
  - Take each team's pool and pour the left-over water out on the ground.
  - The team with the least amount of water left over wins. NOTE: If a team spilled a lot during the race, that water is taken into account along with the amount of water left over in their pool.

- Award points for first to tenth place, according to who has the least water left over.

- Wrestling:
    - Call the first participant of each team to the start line.

    - Thumb wrestling:
        - Have two participants from opposing teams step into the thumb wrestling ring. The opponents must circle each other and then bow.
        - The opponents then step towards each other and give each other their right hand.
        - Assume the wrestling position: Opponents must hold their thumbs up, facing towards the other person. With the rest of their fingertips, the opponents must grab each other's right hand and clasp the two hands together tightly (see image).

        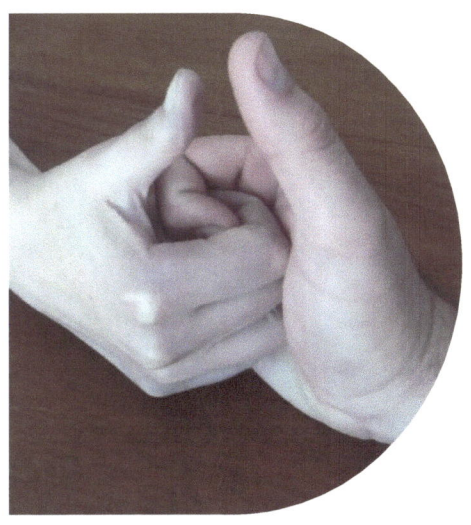

        - Opponents must start each game politely, showing respect by bowing their thumbs to each other. Next, bowing on each count, opponents must chant the following rhyme: "One, two, three, four, I declare a thumb war!"
        - The thumb wrestle begins and each participant must use their thumb to try and pin down their opponent's thumb (see image).
        - Participants are not allowed to lift their elbows away from their bodies.
        - The thumb wrestling ring has to remain vertical at all times.
        - When a participant has managed to pin down their opponent's thumb, they must hold it down for at least four seconds, while chanting, "One, two, three, four, I win the thumb war!"
        - The first participant to pin down their opponent's thumb for four seconds wins.
        - Call the next set of opponents to the thumb wrestle ring.

- Arm-wrestling:
  - Set up a table with two chairs on either side in the middle of the floor.
  - Call two participants from opposing teams to the table. The opponents must circle each other and then bow.
  - The opponents must now take their seats at the table, with their elbows on the table.
  - The opponents are given 30 seconds to take their grip: palm to palm, gripping at the thumbs (see image).
  - The thumb knuckles must be visible and the gripped hands should be level at the forefingers.
  - Explain the following rules:
    - ✓ Participants' free hands must always be on the table.
    - ✓ Participants must keep their shoulders square to the table before the match starts.
    - ✓ The competing elbow must be in contact with the table throughout the match.
    - ✓ The thumb knuckles of the competing hand must be visible before the match starts.
    - ✓ The guide must be able to pass a closed fist between the biceps and forearm of the competing arm before the match starts.
    - ✓ The competing wrists must be straight before the match starts.
    - ✓ The gripped hands must always be in the centre of the table.
    - ✓ Participants' feet must be flat on the floor under the table at all times.
    - ✓ Both participants must keep one buttock on their seat at all times.
  - When the guide gives the signal, the arm-wrestle starts.
  - The first participant to pin down their opponent's arm is the winner.
  - Participants may be disqualified for the following fouls after two warnings:
    - ✓ Participants' shoulders may not cross the centre of the table and must remain in a neutral position.
    - ✓ Participants may not touch any part of their bodies such as their chin, shoulder or head.
    - ✓ Participants may not intentionally push their hand into their opponent's shoulder.
    - ✓ No foul language, poor sportsmanship or abuse is allowed.
    - ✓ The elbow may not lift off the table – not even a little bit.
  - The disqualified participant loses the match.
  - Once a winner is determined, call the next set of opponents to the table.

This grid can be used for all the wrestling challenges. The score works as follows:
10 points for 1st place; 9 points for 2nd place; 8 points for 3rd place, etc.

- Modelling
  - Call the participants of each team forward.
  - If it is a co-ed group, one participant of each team must be male and the other female.
  - The male will play the part of a female model, and the female will play the part of a male model.
  - If it is a single-sex group, the two participants can decide who will be the male and who will be the female.
  - Give the participants one minute to practise their runway walk.
  - When the participants return from their practice, have a table of judges ready. Give the judges fake names and titles, e.g. Mr South Africa 2001.
  - Each team's "male" model must do their runway walk first, followed by the "female" model.
  - The judges must give each couple a score out of 10.
  - Award points for first to tenth place, according to who got the highest score.

- Pop stars
  - All the members of a team must participate.
  - Each team can sing or dance, or combine the two into one performance.
  - Allow each team five minutes to practise.
  - Let each team perform before the same panel of judges as the modelling competition.
  - The judges must give each team a score out of 10.
  - Award points for first to tenth place, according to who got the highest score.

Special rules:
- Each person has to compete in at least one of the events.
- Points may be deducted from teams who make too much noise while other teams are busy competing.
- If you run out of time, you can drop some of the activities that take up a lot of time, e.g. wrestling, modelling, pop stars, etc.

After the session:
- Tally the points on the scoresheet to determine the winning team.
- Gather all the equipment and put it away.
- Leave the area behind clean and neat.

Olympic Scoresheet

		1	2	3	4	5	6	7	8	9	10
Shotput	(1)										
Javelin	(2)										
100 m sprint	(1)										
Hurdles	(2)										
Bowls	(1)										
Bike race	(2)										
Swim	(2)										
Wrestling	(1)										
Modelling	(2)										
Pop stars	(?)										
Totals											

Campfire

You will need:
- Firelighters
- Matches or lighter
- Wood
- Marshmallows
- Sticks for roasting marshmallows.

Site:
- Any outdoor area where it is safe to build a fire.

How it works:
- Let the group join in a singalong session around the campfire.
- Group members can also practise skits to perform at the campfire. These must be two minutes maximum and have a theme, e.g. cartoons, children's rhymes or songs. The skits must adhere to the following rules:
  - Everyone must take part.
  - No racism.
  - No below-the-belt humour – keep it clean.
  - Group members are not allowed to tease or insult each other.
  - Let the group toast marshmallows on sticks.
  - Don't let them burn their sticks in the fire or run around with flaming marshmallows.
  - Be careful and supervise the group closely.
- Let the group tell jokes, but ensure that they are clean jokes.
- Reserve ghost stories for older groups (17+ years).

Rules:
- No horseplay around the fire.
- No one is allowed to poke the fire or put the wood onto the fire except for the facilitators.
- Be careful of embers flying from the fire when new wood is placed on the fire.
- Skits should not happen close to the fire.

After the session:
- Put out the fire properly.
- Put the used marshmallow sticks in water.

Silly Tasks

You will need:
- 1 explanation sheet per team (make laminated copies of the explanation sheet following these instructions)
- 1 x A4 sheet of scrap paper per team
- 1 pencil per team
- Explanation sheets for judges to keep score on (1 per team)
- 1 pencil per judge
- Judges' table and chairs

Site:
- Any comfortable indoor area.

How it works:
- This activity also works as a morning activity or time-filler.
- Divide the group into teams.
- Each team gets 30 minutes to practise their selection. They can use scrap paper and pencils to make notes.
- Set up a judges' table while the teams are practising.
- Call the teams back after the practice time has elapsed.
- Let each team perform one of their activities at a time.
- The judges must give each team a score out of 100 for each activity. In the end, they must add the scores of all the activities together to work out each team's total.
- The team with the highest score wins.

Special rules:
- All team members must take part in the performance.

After the session:
- Collect all the equipment and put it away.
- Place all the scrap paper in a recycling bin, if available.

Silly Tasks

Read through all the tasks carefully before you start.
Your team will receive a score out of 100 for each task, depending on how much effort you put in.

No.	Task	Score
1.	Group hug for 30 seconds.	
2.	The whole team must act out a day in the life of an indigenous tribe.	
3.	Conduct a harmonious one-minute symphony with each team member	
4.	Convince the judges that they are either mad or come from another	
5.	Pretend to cross a 10 m wide acid river	
6.	Disguise a team member effectively so that they blend into their	
7.	Explain to the judges why you think all people should be green.	
8.	Explain to the judges why you think toenails are important and what	
9.	Find an insect and tell the judges more about it.	
10.	Collect as many leaves as you can, put it in a heap and dance around it while singing "Happy earth day to you" to the planet.	
11.	Invent another silly task that is not on this list.	
12.	List as many uses for matches as you can think of.	
13.	Make a hat that fits your guide and convince them to wear it.	
14.	Make a human spiderweb.	
15.	Make up five new letters for the alphabet.	
16.	Make up a rain dance and perform it.	
17.	Make up a rhyme about your stay at the camp.	
18.	Make up a song about an animal to the tune of, "Row, row, row your	
19.	Make up and define five new words, and explain why they are	
20.	One person in your team must talk for one minute without hesitation on	
21.	One person in your team must tell a fairy tale while the others act it out.	
22.	Play a game of basketball with an invisible ball for two minutes.	
23.	Sing one verse from "She'll be coming 'round the mountain" as loud as	
24.	Rap your national anthem.	
25.	Tell the judges a story, with each team member adding one line at a	
26.	Your whole team must do something to make your guide laugh.	
27.	Your whole team must act out any kind of animal.	
28.	Your whole team must form a machine, using only your bodies, which	
29.	Your whole team must do finger aerobics for one minute, without	
30.	Each team member must drink a glass of water upside down in under three minutes. The whole team must do this together.	
31.	Your whole team must act out the Second World War in two minutes.	
32.	Using natural materials, make a cake that looks delicious enough to eat.	
33.	Without saying a word, the whole team must express their experience	
34.	Explain your team's current location, as you would to an alien who has	
35.	Write down one good thing about each team member and present it.	

Constellation Mythology

You will need:
- 1 x A4 sheet of paper per team
- 1 x A3 sheet of black cardboard per team
- 2 pencils per team
- 1 torch per team

Site:
- Any comfortable indoor area or by the campfire.
- This activity can also form part of a night hike. Take a laser pointer with you to point out star constellations.

How it works:
- Explain what a constellation is: a group of stars forming a pattern, which is traditionally named after its apparent form or identified with a mythological figure.
- Each team must draw their own constellation on the A3 cardboard provided. They must make up a story about how their constellation came to be part of the Milky Way.
- The team must act out the scenes as they tell the story.
- Each team can now poke holes in strategic places on the picture of their constellation. Hold it in front of the flashlight so that the light shines through the holes like stars.

After the session:
- Collect all the equipment and put it away.
- Put the used paper and cardboard in a recycling bin, if available.

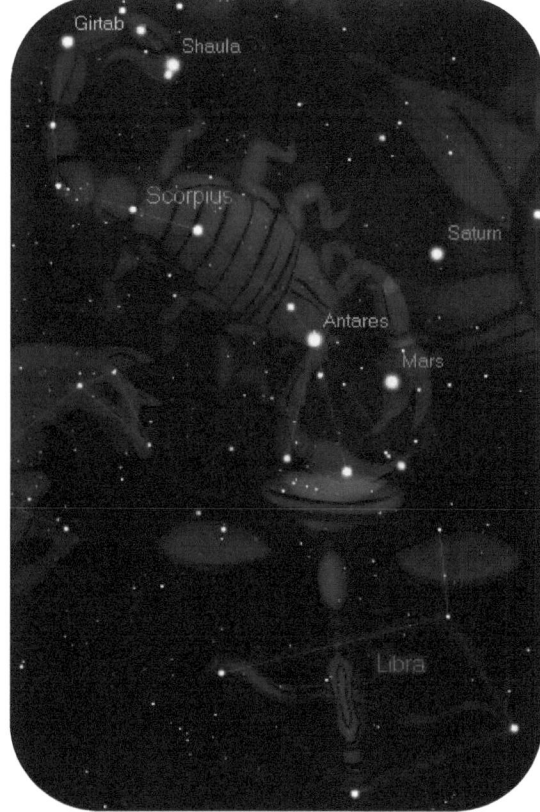

Brain Game

You will need:
- 1 question sheet per team (make laminated copies of the questions following these instructions)
    - Some of the questions in this guide are based on South African general knowledge. You can make up your own questions if you are in a different country.
- 4 x A4 sheets of lined paper per team
- 1 clipboard per team
- 1 pencil per team
- 1 laminated answer sheet for the guide

Site:
- Any comfortable indoor area.

How it works:
- This activity tests the teams' general knowledge.
- Give each team two sheets of lined paper, a clipboard and pencil.
- Start by asking questions 1–13, giving the teams just enough time to write down their answers.
- For question 14, give them the words they need to spell.
- Collect the teams' answers and give them two more sheets of lined paper. Now let them answer the riddle section of this game
- While the teams answer the riddle section of this game, mark their answers for the first section.
- Take in all the papers, question sheets and clipboards.
- The team with the highest number of correct answers wins.

Special rules:
- Teams may not help other teams with answers.

After the session:
- Collect all the equipment and put it away.
- Put any used scrap paper in the recycling bin, if available.

Questions
1. **Name all of the provinces of South Africa.** (9)

Western Cape	Free State	Limpopo
Eastern Cape	North West	Mpumalanga
Northern Cape	Gauteng	KwaZulu-Natal

2. **Name all the countries that share a border with South Africa.** (6)

| Lesotho | Mozambique | Botswana |
| Swaziland | Zimbabwe | Namibia |

3. **Name all the official languages of South Africa.** (11)

English	Northern Sotho	Venda
Afrikaans	Southern Sotho	Tsonga
Zulu	Tswana	Swazi
Xhosa	Ndebele	

(Bonus point for 12th language: sign language) (1)

4. **Name the seven continents on earth.** (7)
Europe, Asia, North America, South America, Australia, Africa, Antarctica

5. **Name the original planets that made up our solar system, in order from the sun.** (9)
Mercury, Venus, Earth, Mars, Jupiter, Saturn, Uranus, Neptune, Pluto

6. **Name the colours of the South African flag.** (6)
Green, blue, red, white, black, yellow

7. **If the flag is hoisted, which colour is at the top?** (1)
Red

8. **Name South Africa's national:** (5)
8.1 Saltwater fish: Galjoen (black bream/blackfish). Bonus point for freshwater fish: Yellowfish
8.2 Tree: Yellowwood tree
8.3 Bird: Blue crane
8.4 Flower: King protea
8.5 Animal: Springbok

9. Name South Africa's Big Five animals. (5)

Lion　　　　　　　　　Rhino　　　　　　　　Buffalo
Leopard　　　　　　　Elephant

10. Name the indigenous animals and plants that feature on South African coins. (7)

5c - Blue crane
10c - Arum lily/"varkoor"
20c - King protea
50c - Strelitzia
R1 - Springbok
R2 - Kudu
R5 - Black wildebeest

(Two bonus points for older coins: 1c - Mossie/Cape sparrow; 2c - Fish eagle or blue wildebeest)

11. Name the capital city of : (3)

11.1　Australia　　=　Canberra
11.2　Zambia　　　=　Lusaka
11.3　Egypt　　　　=　Cairo

12. Which is the longest river in South Africa and how long is it? (2)
Orange River, 2 200 km

13. Which is the highest mountain in Africa and in which country does most of it lie? (2)
Mount Kilimanjaro, Tanzania

14. Spell the following words: (6)
14.1 Hippopotamus
14.2 Mississippi
14.3 Diarrhoea
14.4 Cappuccino
14.5 Rhinoceros
14.6 Xylophone
(Bonus points for: schizophrenic; gynaecologist)

Total (80)

Riddles

1. **You are standing behind your father and at the same time he is standing behind you, how can this be possible?**
You are standing back to back.

2. **You throw a ball as hard as you can. It does not hit anything and it is not thrown back to you by anyone. After a little while, you catch it again. How is this possible?**
You threw the ball up in the air.

3. **There is a washing machine with white socks and red socks inside. Maximum how many times should you stick your hand in and pull out one sock at a time until you have a matching pair?**
Three times (white, red, white/red, white, red).
OR
Two times, as the colours have run together and all the socks are now pink.

4. **A man runs a lap in one and a half minutes. Another man runs the same lap in 90 seconds. Who is the winner?**
They completed the lap at the same time.

5. **You are in a race and overtake the person in second place. What position are you in?**
Second.

6. **An electric train travels at 100 km/h in a north-easterly direction. After five minutes, it changes direction and heads in a south-easterly direction at 85 km/h. After another five minutes, it changes direction again and heads in a south-westerly direction at 110 km/h. In which direction is the train's smoke travelling?**
Electric trains do not produce smoke.

7. **How far into a forest do you need to walk until you start walking back out?**
Halfway.

8. **Fit TEN HORSES into the nine open spaces below:**

T	E	N	H	O	R	S	E	S

9. **What weighs more: a kilogram of feathers or a kilogram of bricks?**
They weigh the same.

10. **A man and his son are travelling in a car and have a serious accident. The man is killed instantly and the son is rushed to the hospital. The son is taken straight into emergency surgery. The surgeon walks in and upon**

> seeing the boy lying on the table says, "I can't operate. This boy is my son." How is this possible?

The surgeon is the boy's mother.

11. There are 20 blackbirds in the tree. The farmer takes his shotgun and shoots one blackbird. How many birds are left in the tree?

None – they all flew away after the shot.

12. My name starts with "t", ends with "t", and has "t" in the middle. What am I?

Teapot

13. What is nailed shut, only used once, never seen while being used, and used for a very long time?

Coffin

14. If a rooster sits on a 45-degree roof facing north and the wind is blowing in a south-westerly direction, in which direction will an egg roll if it is laid on top of the roof?

Roosters don't lay eggs.

15. A cowboy rides into town on Friday stays two nights and rides out on Friday. How is this possible?

His horse is named Friday.

16. A man is walking down the road dressed entirely in black. There are no lights on anywhere and no moonlight. A car with no lights comes down the road and manages to avoid the man. How?

It is daylight.

17. You are in a cabin with four walls, all facing north. There is a bear outside. What colour is the bear?

White – you are in the South Pole.

18. You walk into a room with only one match. You must light a lantern, a gas stove, a candle, the fire in the fireplace and the pilot light of the water heater. What do you light first?

The match

19. What occurs once in a minute, twice in a moment but never in an hour?

The letter "m".

20. What question can you never answer yes to?

Are you asleep?

Evening Solitaire

See the instructions for solitaire under "Day Activities".

Evening Orienteering

See the instructions for orienteering under "Day Activities".

Battle of the Bands

You will need:
- Coloured paper, scissors and colouring pencils

Site:
- Indoor area.

How it works:
- Each team must come up with their own band name. They must also compose and perform an original song.
- Each team must design a CD cover, using the paper, pencils and scissors.
- Give the teams a set time in which they will have to prepare for their performance.
- This game is great for rainy days.

Special rules:
- Teams may not use existing songs.
- All team members must participate.

After the session:
- Collect all the equipment and put it away.
- Place any paper off-cuts in the recycling bin, if available.

Litter Busters

You will need:
- Box with clean waste items such as bottle caps, plastic bottles, screws, nails, pieces of wood, plastic bags, straws, pieces of rope and any other items lying around.

Site:
- Indoor area.

How it works:
- Depending on time, you can play any or all of the stages of this game.
- Show the teams what kinds of items are in their boxes.
- Give the teams a set amount of time to complete any or all of the following tasks, using the litter in their boxes:
    - Each team must pick a member to be their litter model. They must create the following for their model: shoes, clothes and a hat. They have to dazzle with creativity and style.
    - Each team must practise and perform a play or a song about litter.
    - Each team must build one of the following things (the guide's choice):
        - Robot
        - Musical instrument
        - Key holder
        - Cleaning supplies
        - Open category
        - Flowerpot or candleholder
- When they're done, the teams can showcase their items to the rest of the group.

Special rules:
- The teams may only use the items in their boxes.

After the session:
- Discuss recycling and possible ways to reuse items with the group.
- Collect all the waste items, put it back in the boxes and store it away.

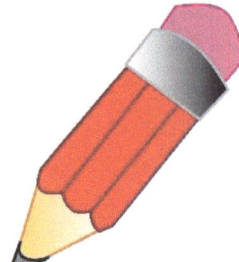

Litter Busters

Task 1
- As a team, pick a member to be your litter model.
- Make the following items for your model:
  - Shoes
  - Clothing
  - Hat
- Once they are dressed, your model must "trash" the runway with style and creativity.

Task 2
- Your team must practise and perform a song or play about litter.

Task 3
- Your team must build one of the following items, as instructed by your guide:
  - Robot
  - Musical instrument
  - Key holder
  - Cleaning supplies
  - Open category
  - Flowerpot or candleholder

Stalk the Lantern

You will need:
- 1 lantern or torch
- 1 whistle
- 1 bright torch per guide

Site:
- Open field at night.

How it works:
- While the group goes for a short walk around the camp, select a spot in the field and set up the lantern on a rock.
- Explain to the group how the game works:
    - Group members have to try to get close enough to touch the lantern without being spotted by the guides.
    - If a guide spots a group member, they will shine their torch on the member, who must then go back to the starting point and try again.
    - Group members are not allowed to run, as it is dark and they might trip and get hurt.
    - Group members are not allowed to throw rocks into the bushes to try and see where the guides are hiding.
    - A blow on the whistle indicates the end of the activity and that everyone has to make their way back to camp.
- Once you've explained the rules, all the guides must go find a hiding spot from where they can see the lantern.

After the session:
- Collect all the equipment and put it away.
- Count all the group members and make sure that no one was left behind in the dark.

Playing Drums

You will need:
- A set of drums
    - If you don't have drums, cut flaps in the bottoms of old, empty refrigerant cylinders and use them as drums (see images).

Site:
- Outdoor area or by the campfire.

How it works:
- Play the drums as accompaniment for songs and role play activities.
- Instruct the group to hold their drums tightly between their legs.
- Use a flat hand to beat the drum, hitting it with your palm.
- The sides of the drum also produce sound.

Special rules:
- If you don't have a drum for each group member, let them share.
- The group may only play their drums when instructed to do so.
- There are sharp edges on the drums, so group members must be careful when holding it between their knees and thighs.

After the session:
- Collect the drums and put them away.

Environmental Activities

Water Testing

You will need:
- 1 water testing kit per team
    - Make sure the kit contains all the necessary equipment, including a manual with instructions and detailed descriptions.

Site:
- Indoor area for testing tap water.
- Outdoor area with a water source nearby, e.g. river, stream or dam.

How it works:
- Divide the group in4 to teams, and give each team a water testing kit. Explain to the teams that they must use their kit to test the clarity or turbidity (murkiness) of the water from the tap or natural source.
- The testing kit will reveal the number of particles in the water, which will give the teams an indication of the clarity of the water.
- The teams must also test the temperature and dissolved oxygen to determine whether fish and plants could survive in the water.
- Next, the teams must test the pH levels of the water, which will reveal the acid/alkaline levels and basic quality of the water.
- Each team must write down their results.
- Discuss the results with the teams and ask them whether animals and plants would be able to live in the water.

Special rules:
- A guide must be present at all times.
- Ensure the teams' safety by the waterside.
- Once a team has collected water from the source, they must move away from the source for testing.

After the session:
- Collect all the testing kits and make sure each of them contains all their elements.
- Rinse the test kits with fresh water, let them dry and put them away.

Sustainable Technologies

In this section, you will find examples of available sustainable technologies. Find technologies that are available in your area and build your programme with those technologies.

Examples of sustainable technologies:
- Iketela
- Stovetec
- Sun stove
- Parabolic solar cooker
- Wonderbag
- Hotbag
- Paper brick maker
- Glass-cutting equipment
- Etc.

Site:
Any spacious area.

How it works:
- Here are some examples of sustainable technologies that you could demonstrate to the group:

    o Iketela: The Iketela is a uniquely designed kettle that quickly boils water using coal and bits of wood or other natural fuel. The kettle comprises a double-skinned wall that holds water around a central open chimney. This kettle design takes the basic science of heating water in a pot and amplifies the use of the heat source in order to boost efficiency. In a normal pot over a fire scenario, the heat source will heat the bottom of the pot. The water in direct contact of the bottom of the pot will heat up and rise. Then the "new" colder water takes the place of the hot water and the bottom of the pot heats that water as well. This continues until all the water is hot. By making a chimney in the middle of the kettle to increase the surface area, the surface exposed to the heat (which is in contact with the water) is increased. This speeds up the heating process. The Iketela boils 7 l of water in approximately seven minutes on an open fire.

- Stovetec: The top is made of cast iron. The stove is lined with ceramic material and well insulated. The ceramic side walls conduct heat very poorly and thus regulate the heat through the centre upwards for maximum efficiency. Consequently, the heat is not lost but rather forced upwards to the cooking surface.

- Sun stove: The sun stove is a highly effective solar cooker. Sun beams containing a heat source reflect on the inner walls of the stove and bounce around within. This action heats up whatever is placed inside. Dark pots or pans work best. The transparent lid creates a super-powered greenhouse effect.

- Parabolic solar cooker: The parabolic solar cooker has a diameter of almost 1.5 m, which produces a high output of energy (heat) for very efficient cooking using only solar power. The focus point of the sun's rays comes together at about 70 cm above the middle or bottom of the parabola. The sun's heat rays reflect against the shiny sides and focus on the pot. 200 degrees Celsius is reached within one second of turning the dish to the sun.

- Wonderbag: The Wonderbag is a simple but revolutionary portable, non-electric slow cooker. Wonderbag's clever insulation allows food that has been brought to the boil to continue slow cooking in the bag for up to 12 hours. The Wonderbag consists of an inner layer of insulation containing recycled polystyrene balls / foam chips, with an outer, draw-string covering of poly-cotton textiles. The Wonderbag was designed by a South African woman, Sarah Collins.

- Hotbag: The Hotbag can be used the same way as the Wonderbag, but is better at keeping food hot while waiting for serving time. A Hotbag is an insulated bag that uses retained heat to cook or steam any food that normally cooks with water. Once you have started cooking on the stove, slip your boiling-hot pot of food into the Hotbag. The bag is made from poly-cotton textiles with two thin layers of isolation wool sandwiching a sheet of heat reflecting film (similar to that of an emergency blanket). It continues to cook on the kitchen counter beside your stove, thereby saving fuel or electricity.

- Can-press: The Can-press does exactly what its name says. It presses cans so that they take up less space. This allows you to put more cans into a container for recycling.

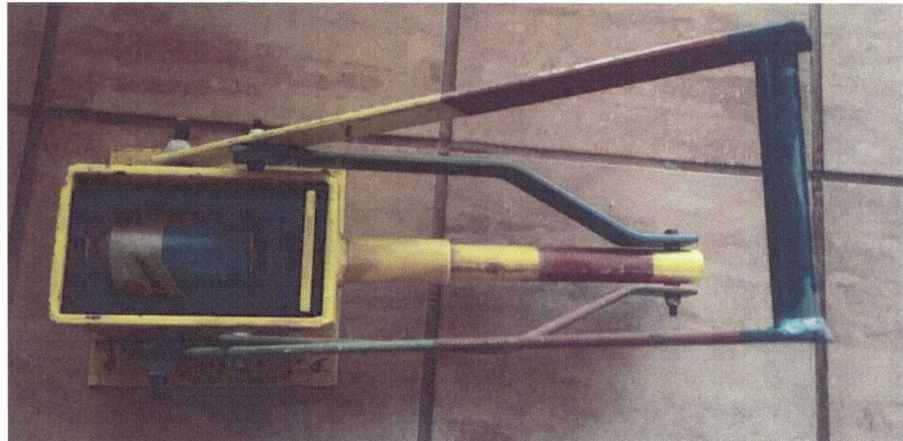

- Paper brickmaker: Paper bricks are a good way to reuse paper and can be used to light fires. Soak a pack of shredded or scrunched-up paper in a bucket of water. Take out the paper and fill your brick maker with it. Put the top plate in and squash out all the water, making sure that the paper is as compact as possible. Remove the paper brick and place it outside in the sun to dry.

- Geyser blankets: By insulating the geyser against normal heat loss through the steel casing, the geyser blanket keeps your hot water hot for longer – meaning your geyser won't switch on as often, saving you energy and money. Because hot-water electricity use comprises around 40% of a typical household's consumption, it is important to reduce heat losses in this area. Often geyser water temperature will drop by 1°C per hour, so constant energy is needed to maintain the temperature. This blanket can cut energy use by half.

- Red wiggler worms/worm tea: When worm tea is used as plant food it can be diluted 50/50 with water and applied with each watering, or it can be applied full strength once a week with water application between each use. Worm tea does not heat up and will not burn your plants. Your plants will absorb the nutrients in the worm tea and castings when they are ready to use it. Worm tea will repopulate the soil with microbes, enrich the roots and break down the thatch, turning it into food for the grass. Worm tea applied as a foliar spray will act as a fertiliser. Plants will produce more foliage and larger stems. This is a good treatment for plants that are stressed or lacking enough sun. To use as a repellent spray, plant liberally with full-strength worm tea, and apply again after it rains. Watering plants with worm tea naturally repel aphids, spider mites, scale and white flies. Worm tea is the liquid that runs from a worm farm, i.e. the liquid produced by the worms.

- Roof tornados: A roof tornado provides positive extraction, which removes heat, fumes, steam and dust. It improves productivity and indoor air quality. It is also bird- and waterproof.

- Glass cutting:

    - Step 1: Fill a large pot with warm water. This will be your bottle's hot bath. Bring the water to boil, and then reduce to a simmer. You can start this before you cut your bottle so that it is ready by the time your bottle is scored (see step 3).

    - Step 2: Fill another large pot with cold water and add enough ice to cover the top of the water. This will be your bottle's cold bath. You will want this pot very close to the hot bath for easy transfers.

    - Step 3: Take a wine bottle and peel all the labels off, using a razor blade. Make a thin score line on the bottle with a cutter: Put the top of a cutter into the mouth of the bottle to stabilise it, and adjust the arms on the cutter so that the blade hits the bottle where you'd like it cut. Tighten all of the bolts to ensure that the arms are stable and in place. Holding your right hand over the stabilising arm and the cutter, left hand on the bottle, touch the cutter with light pressure to the wine bottle. Slowly turn the wine bottle with your left hand, making sure to create as much of a continuous motion as possible. A thin score line will appear on the bottle (you should hear and see it). DO NOT continue to go over the scoreline once you have gone around the bottle. The thinner the line, the better. If you missed a spot, ONLY go back over that spot, not the rest of the line.

- Step 4: Place the bottle (scoreline submerged) into the warm bath. Make sure that the scoreline is completely submerged, and leave it for about 5–8 seconds. Then move the bottle to the cold bath for another 5–8 seconds. Repeat this process until your bottle breaks. You will hear and see it crack along the scoreline. Be gentle enough with the bottle while transferring it between pots so as not to bang the bottle on the bottom or sides of the pots. The bottle will break in either the warm or cold bath, so make sure to have tongs handy in case it happens in the hot bath!

- Step 5: Once your bottle breaks, clean up the edges with sandpaper. Using sandpaper, go around the front and inside edges with the paper, knocking off any "burs" left from cutting. This will smooth the edges and give it a more finished look. Make sure you do this in an area that can be easily cleaned, such as over the sink, to avoid shards of glass landing everywhere on your floor.

After the session:
- Clean all the equipment and put it away.

Enviromeal

You will need:
- 1 tub or crate per team, containing the following:
  - 1 measuring jug
  - 1 cutting board
  - 1 grater
  - 1 wooden spoon
  - 1 plastic spoon
  - 1 egg lifter
  - 1 whisk
  - 1 tong
  - 1 teaspoon
  - 2 spoons for dishing
  - 2 knives
  - 1 small knife
  - 1 x 5 l container
  - 1 x 2 l container
  - 1 x 250 ml container
  - 2 mixing bowls
  - 1 dishing bowl
  - 2 big dishing bowls
  - 1 strainer
  - 1 pan
  - 4 material shopping bags
  - A set of colouring pencils
  - Writing paper

How it works:
- Divide the group into small teams, who will have to prepare their own meals.
- Go through the instructions on the explanation sheet with the teams (the explanation sheet follows these instructions).

Special rules:
- Teams must prepare their meals in the most eco-friendly way possible.
- The more eco-friendly their methods, the more points will be deducted from a team. The less eco-friendly their methods, the more points will be given to a team, e.g.:
  - Points will be given for using plastic bags (not eco-friendly).
  - Points will be deducted for using the material bag provided in the tub (more eco-friendly).
  - The group with the least points against their name will be the winners.

After the session:
- Do an inventory of all the boxes to ensure that nothing is missing from the contents.
- Put all the equipment away.

Enviromeal Activity Sheet

How it works:
- This activity examines some of the choices we make as consumers, in particular choices around food, packaging and waste, which have an impact on our environment.
- Your team must plan and prepare a meal, which you will eat together.
- You will need to purchase all the ingredients you need for the meal with the money provided by the guides.
- Afterwards, your meal will be audited to assess its environmental impact in terms of food types, travelling, cooking method and packaging. The enviromeal auditing sheet will be used for this purpose.
- Your team's final score represents the impact of your meal on the environment. The higher the score, the greater the impact.
- Scores are calculated as follows:
  - Each kilometre you travel to purchase your food will add points to your score. The further you travel, the greater the impact on the environment.
  - Each item of packaging earns packaging points. Some types of packaging can be recycled or reused and are considered to have a lower environmental impact than non-recyclable types; e.g. composite packaging, which consists of many layers of different materials (wax, plastic, foil, paper, etc.), has a greater impact than cardboard.
  - Food types are also scored. Foods further up the food chain (e.g. meat and fish) earn higher points than foods further down the food chain (e.g. vegetables and fruit), because their production requires higher inputs of energy, resources and land.
  - The method of cooking could have a very big impact on the environment – either directly in the form of pollution or indirectly through the way it is manufactured or harvested. Therefore, your cooking methods will also be scored.
- The only ingredients provided beforehand are:
  - Salt
  - Selected spices
  - Oil
  - Water

Special rules:
- The only ingredients that will be provided are the once stated above. You need to purchase everything else you will require to prepare and serve your food, including tomato sauce, drinks, etc.
- You may NOT add your own money to the money provided. You must remain within your budget.
- Your team should attempt to cater for the preferences and special dietary requirements of all its members.
- Teams may not exchange or purchase items from other teams.
- You may not purchase precooked foods such as roast chicken, pies or pizza.

- You may not purchase half-cooked foods such as two-minute noodles or other instant foods.
- You may not remove any packaging from items while shopping in order to reduce your packaging points.
- Collect and keep all items of packaging which came with your ingredients – nothing may be discarded.
- All purchases should be accompanied by till slips. Keep these for auditing purposes.
- Each team should cater for their guide and one of the other facilitators, and invite them to eat with the team.
- You will have 20 minutes to plan your meal.
- Four members of your team must be sent to do the shopping. They will have one hour.
- Upon the shoppers' return to base camp, your team must prepare your food, set the tables and make invitations and menus.
- The team members who did not go shopping may get a head start on the tables, invitations and menus.

Auditing the meals (guide to make copies of the auditing sheet and complete one for each team):
- Make a list of all items purchased and their prices.
- Calculate how much money was spent and how much was left over.
- Separate the packaging into types, according to the enviromeal auditing sheet. Count how many pieces of each type of packaging are present; e.g. if you have two soft plastic bags, each bag will receive a packaging point.
- Calculate a subtotal for packaging.
- Identify the food types that are present. Calculate a subtotal for food types.
- Work out the kilometres travelled. Take into account the type of car used. Calculate a subtotal for transport.
- Identify the method of cooking and calculate a subtotal for cooking methods.
- Calculate the bonus points.
- Add all the subtotals together and subtract the bonus points to get the grand total.
- Interpret the meal's environmental impact according to the score.

ENVIROMEAL AUDIT SHEET

Category : TRAVEL
Distance travelled as a group.

Kilometres	Score
0,5	0,5
1	1
1,5	1,5
2	2
2,5	2,5
3	3
3,5	3,5
4	4
4,5	4,5
5	5
	Subtotal 1

Basicaly 1 point per kilometre
Intervals of 0.5

Type of vehicle	Score
Car	3
Minibus	2
Bus	1
	Subtotal 2

Category : COOKING METHOD

Sun	0
Wood	2
Coal	3
Gas	4
Electricity	5
	Subtotal 3

Category : PACKAGING

Items	Score	x of items	Score
Returnable glass bottle	1		
Reusable container	2		
Paper/cardboard	1		
Tin	3		
Can/aluminium	2		
Soft plastic	4		
Hard plastic	3		
Styrofoam/polystyrene	5		
		Subtotal 4	

Category : FOOD TYPES

Items	Score
Red meat	5
Chicken / pork	3
Fish	4
Veg	1
Fruit / salad	1
Bread / rice	2
Pasta	2
Maize meal	2
Tinned food	4
Custard & cheese	4
Ice cream	4
	Subtotal 5

Category : BEVERAGES

Pure fruit juice	1
Bottled water	2
Juice concentrate	3
Tea/coffee	2
Milk	2
Alcohol	6
Fizzy drinks	5
	Subtotal 6

Bonus points (-)

Presentation	1,2,3
Healthy/nutrition	1,2,3
Teamwork	1,2,3
Cleaning	1,2,3

Bonus total

Bonus points (-)

Stovetec	-1
Hotbag	-1
Other technologies	-1

Bonus points (-)
Change left over

R0 - R10	-1
R10 - R20	-2
R20 - R30	-3
R40 - R50	-4
R50 +	-5
If over budget	+ 5

Interpretation

20-50	Eco-stars
51-70	hmmmmm
71 +	Disa-stars

Total score	1	2	3	4	5	6	subtotal	min	=

92

Camping Out

Camping Out

You will need:
- 1 tub containing the following:
    - 3 toilet paper rolls
    - 1 toilet bin
    - Brown sanitary paper bags (one for each girl)
    - 2 bottles of liquid hand soap
    - 1 bottle of dishwashing liquid
    - 2 scorers
    - 1 box of matches
    - 1 box of firelighters
    - 3 black dustbin bags
- Spare gas-lamp mantle
- 2 large basins for washing dishes
- 2 small basins for washing hands
- 2 plastic camping tables
- 1 gas lamp with gas bottle and extension
- Enough tents for the group (put them up the day before the campout)
- For cooking:
    - Enough cutlery
    - 1 dishcloth
    - Enough water containers filled with drinking water
    - 4 cans filled with water for cleaning and fire extinguishing
    - Food
        - See Book 1 in this series (*Cooking for a Camp, Hostel or Large Group*) for meal suggestions.

Pre-camp preparation:
- Assemble the tents.
- Prepare the campsite's toilet / ablution facilities. Add sanitary bags, toilet paper and a bin.
- Make sure there is enough campfire wood.

Site:
- A suitable campsite.

How it works:
- Gather the group.
- Tell them to go pack for camp. They must pack as light as possible, because they are only sleeping out for one night and they have to carry all their things themselves.
- Start walking to the campsite.
- Ask an assistant to drive the food to the campsite and to light a fire when they get there.
- When you arrive at the campsite with the group, assign them their tents. Let them roll out their sleeping bags in the tents and settle in while it is still light outside.
- Show the group where the toilet is.
- While the group members are busy settling in, start setting up for dinner.
- Fill the basins for the group members to wash their hands.
- Call the group together for dinner.
- Make sure all group members behave themselves around the fire.

Special rules:
- Group members are not allowed to push and shove one another around the campfire, as this might be dangerous.
- Group members may not put more wood on the fire or play with the fire.
- No one is allowed near any water sources in the area.
- Only firewood may be thrown on the fire – no other items.
- Group members must not mess in the tents, as they will have to clean them before hiking back in the morning.
- No horseplay is allowed in the tents.
- No one is allowed to play with the tent zippers, flaps, pegs or ropes.

After the session:
- Group members must clean out their tents.
- Clean and pack away all the equipment, including the food.
- Do an inventory to ensure that no equipment is missing.
- Ensure that the campsite is left behind clean and neat.